Seattle Slew

Also Available from Eclipse Press

THOROUGHBRED
Legends®

Seattle Slew

Racing's First Undefeated
Triple Crown Winner

D AN M EARNS

**ECLIPSE
PRESS**

Essex, Connecticut

**ECLIPSE
PRESS**

An imprint of Globe Pequot, the trade division of
The Rowman & Littlefield Publishing Group, Inc.
4501 Forbes Blvd., Ste. 200
Lanham, MD 20706
www.rowman.com

Distributed by NATIONAL BOOK NETWORK

British Library Cataloguing in Publication Information available

Library of Congress Cataloging-in-Publication Data available

ISBN 978-1-4930-8068-7 (paperback)
ISBN 978-1-4930-8069-4 (ebook)

♾™ The paper used in this publication meets the minimum requirements
of American National Standard for Information Sciences—Permanence of
Paper for Printed Library Materials, ANSI/NISO Z39.48-1992.

CONTENTS

SEATTLE SLEW

INTRODUCTION

An Unlikely Hero

This is the story of a hero who rose from humble beginnings to become one of the greatest race-horses of the 20th Century, overcoming tremendous obstacles along the way. His fairy tale story has been likened to Cinderella and the Ugly Duckling — an unremarkable foal, sold cheaply as a yearling, who became a king under bridle and saddle — and could have been penned by Horatio Alger.

This is a Kentucky story. Foaled in the Bluegrass, he won the state's signature race, the Kentucky Derby, then later returned to Kentucky to achieve glory as a stallion.

It is also a New York story. Based there throughout his racing career, he won some of his greatest races in the Big Apple, completing the Triple Crown at Belmont Park and acquiring a legion of vocal followers in a place where fans can sometimes seem jaded and mean.

Add in touches of Maryland, Florida, Washington, and foreign outposts, where Slew's offspring later made their mark, to the story's geographic mix.

This is the story of a horse surrounded by controversy as surely as flies swirl about the muck pile.

It is the story of a horse who survived a near-death experience and came back better and faster than ever...a horse who entered stud at the right farm at the wrong time, yet became one of the premier American Thoroughbred stallions of the latter 20th Century.

It is the story of a horse whose achievements on the track and in the breeding shed will be remembered and recalled with admiration and respect...a horse whose name will shine forever in the annals of racing history.

It is the story of a horse called Slew.

Dan Mearns
Punta Gorda, Florida, 2000

CHAPTER I

Baby Huey

Based on looks and lineage, Seattle Slew at birth could not have been termed a horse destined for greatness.

"He was ugly," Paul Mallory recalled of the nearly black colt foaled the day after Valentine's Day, 1974, at breeder Ben Castleman's small Kentucky farm. "He had big ears, and they flopped all over for the first week."[1]

Mallory managed Castleman's 100-acre White Horse Acres Farm near Lexington, and both he and his wife, Christine, participated in Seattle Slew's foaling. Christine had a kinder view of the flop-eared foal.

"Move over and let me take a picture of this Derby winner," she told her husband in an eerily prescient remark.

"He looks more like a mule to me," Mallory replied.

The racing world was still abuzz that winter about

the achievements of Secretariat, who the previous year had ended a twenty-five-year drought by becoming the sport's first Triple Crown winner since Citation. While the odds of another Triple Crown winner's being foaled just one year later were astronomical, every breeder had hopes that his or her new foal would follow in Secretariat's hoof prints. This was particularly true among breeders whose foals were related, albeit remotely, to the Meadow Stable champion.

Castleman's new foal, a plain, dark bay colt with no white markings, seemed the antithesis of Secretariat. The latter was a gorgeous chestnut with a white "star" and "stripe" on his forehead and three white "stockings," the only horse deemed worthy to share the sacred nickname of Man o' War — Big Red.

The new foal indeed was distantly related to Secretariat, through the blood of Secretariat's sire Bold Ruler, but it was diluted through Boldnesian, a much less successful son of Bold Ruler, and again through Boldnesian's son Bold Reasoning. The names of other great horses likewise appeared in the foal's family tree — War Admiral, Blue Larkspur, Equipoise, Round Table — but they, too, were generations removed.

Castleman had purchased White Horse Acres in 1960, naming the farm after his popular restaurant, White Horse Tavern, in northern Kentucky, near Cincinnati. A longtime gathering place for horsemen from Latonia Racetrack (now Turfway Park) in Florence, Kentucky, the restaurant's walls were crowded with winner's circle photos supplied by owners and trainers. Their influence rubbed off on Castleman, who became a Thoroughbred owner in the mid-1950s.

Castleman had wanted to breed Seattle Slew's dam, My Charmer, to a Bold Ruler-line stallion. Bold Ruler had died of cancer in July of 1971, when Secretariat was a yearling, but the great stallion left many sons to carry on his legacy. My Charmer was Castleman's best horse, and he thought she would be an excellent producer. He wanted only the best for his adored mare, who had won the Fair Grounds Oaks in Castleman's color and was a daughter of his foundation mare, Fair Charmer.

So Castleman sought the advice of Seth Hancock, president of historic Claiborne Farm in Paris, Kentucky, where Bold Ruler had stood at stud. Hancock, who was in the process of syndicating Secretariat for stud duty at

Claiborne, advised Castleman to try Bold Reasoning, who was standing his first breeding season at the farm for a stud fee of $5,000.

Bold Reasoning had been a tough, hard-luck race-horse. When he was good, he was very good, winning the Jersey Derby and Withers Stakes as a three-year-old and setting a track record of 1:08 4/5 for six furlongs at Belmont Park. A series of throat and leg disorders, however, kept him from performing at consistently high levels.

The result of Hancock's suggested mating was a strong, bullish foal who quickly became the leader among the half-dozen young horses born at White Horse in 1974.

"He was the boss, even when he was little," Mallory recalled. "Didn't nobody bother him while he was eating."[2]

The precocious My Charmer colt remained a handful for the Mallorys through his weanling and yearling seasons. By the time of his first official birthday (January 1, as it is for all Thoroughbreds in the Northern Hemisphere), he weighed 700 pounds.

Castleman attempted to place him in the 1975 Keeneland summer yearling sale, the most important

auction of its kind in the world, but sale officials rejected the colt based on pedigree and appearance. Instead,
the colt became one of two young horses Castleman
nominated to the Lexington auction conducted by
Fasig-Tipton Company, then in its second year of com-
peting with the premier Keeneland sale.

The New York Times writer Steve Cady, in his 1977
book on Seattle Slew, quoted the assessment of the My
Charmer colt made by Ted Bates of Fasig-Tipton:

"Above average in size — shoulder developed well
— good angle and strong back — good through the
middle, with good spring of rib — nice hind leg, but
passes close at hocks — quick appearance — turns out
moderately right front from knee down."

Significantly, Bates also noted that the angling out
of the right front hoof, a condition known to horsemen
as toeing-out, "should not preclude a racing career."

Mallory had a knack for getting yearlings ready for
sales, and the colt was on his best behavior, his coat
shining, when he took up residence in one of the stalls
at Fasig-Tipton's Newtown Paddocks sale grounds.
Mallory had done his best with the colt, but the young
animal still seemed coarse and awkward, and the toeing

out was seen by some as a serious conformational defect.

Few potential buyers showed up for a pre-sale look. Among those who did stop by was prominent trainer LeRoy Jolley, who asked Mallory to bring out the colt, then issued a curt "put him back" upon surveying the prospect. But beauty, especially when it concerns Thoroughbred conformation, is in the eye of the beholder, and someone apparently had taken a liking to the colt. When he went through the sale ring, bidding stopped at $17,500. Not much, but more than Mallory thought the colt would bring. Castleman had told the farm manager not to let the colt go if he brought less than $15,000.[3]

The winning bid was higher than the Fasig-Tipton average price of $10,683, but well below the averages for that year's Keeneland summer sale ($53,637) and Fasig-Tipton Saratoga sale ($37,068). The buyer was listed as Pearson's Barn out of Washington State.

If anyone had bothered to check, he or she would have found the new owners of the My Charmer colt to be relative newcomers to the Thoroughbred scene, but their modest purchase ultimately would make them household names.

The owners, who came to be known as the Slew Crew, were a young, delightful pair of thirtysomething married couples, Mickey and Karen Taylor and Jim and Sally Hill. Coming on the heels of the adorable Penny Chenery, owner of Secretariat, the Slew Crew seemed to have been ordered from the same "good owner" catalog by the sport of racing.

The Taylors, former high school sweethearts, lived in south central Washington. Mickey, a fourth-generation lumberman, had started his own lumber business in 1972, and Karen worked as a flight attendant for Northwest Orient Airlines. Taylor had long been a racing fan, and a series of timely investments and soaring pulp prices in the Northwest in the 1970s allowed him the luxury of promising Karen a racehorse for their third anniversary. Despite their newfound wealth, however, the couple continued to live in a mobile home in White Swan, a town of 600 located in the middle of the Yakima Indian Reservation.

Karen's gift horse, purchased through an acquaintance, never started, but the Taylors remained undaunted. They got their first victory, in December of 1973, with a gelding named Triangular, whom they had bought for $55,000 from trainer Allen Jerkens in New York. Shipped to California, Triangular won three of his first four races for the couple, including a grade III stakes, and the Taylors were hooked.

More importantly, they teamed up with Jim Hill, a veterinarian who lived with his wife Sally in Garden City, New York, and wintered in Florida. On the advice of a mutual friend (Dr. Bob Penney), Taylor had Hill act as agent in the purchase of Triangular.

The Hills had met at Auburn University in Alabama, where Hill went to veterinary school. He also had spent time as a cowboy and rodeo rider. Sally was the daughter of an Air Force colonel and the niece of Sanders Russell, who drove A.C.'s Viking to victory in harness racing's premier event, the Hambletonian.

Hill and Taylor did not actually meet until 1974, when they ran into each other at a newspaper-vending machine outside the Campbell House Inn in Lexington, Kentucky. They struck up a friendship, and Hill began recommending horses for the Taylors at yearling sales, where he picked out Seattle Slew.

"When I first saw him, I said he was a runner or my name was not Jim Hill," he recalled. "I thought he had everything it took, from a physical standpoint, to be a racehorse. I certainly didn't foresee he would be a champion, but I did feel he would be a runner."[4]

In Hill's eyes, Slew possessed powerful shoulders and the kind of straight angles in his legs, back, head, and neck that indicate racing aptitude. Hill had done veterinary work on Bold Reasoning and performed fertility tests on Slew's sire after the horse retired from racing. He thought Seattle Slew was the best of Bold Reasoning's first-crop yearlings entered in the sale.

"I had an edge because I knew Bold Reasoning was a special horse," Hill later recalled. "He operated with a lot of disabilities and things beyond his control."[5]

Hill had to leave Lexington before the sale to operate on a horse in New York. Taylor drove the Hills to the airport, where Hill advised his new partner, "Do whatever it takes to get the Bold Reasoning colt. We really want him."

It didn't take much convincing, because the Taylors also wanted the colt, albeit for less pragmatic reasons.

"He had a lot of pizzazz to him," Taylor said. "Karen really fell in love with him."

Taylor and Hill expected to get the colt for $12,000

or $13,000, but the bidding went higher. Taylor stayed in, remembering Hill's admonition while feeling Karen's elbow poking him in the ribs, and purchased the colt for $17,500.

Taylor called Hill that night in New York.

"Did we get him?" was Hill's first question.

"After he hung up," Sally Hill recalled, "he said to me, 'I think we bought a champion.' Both of us kind of laughed."[6]

In 1974, the Hills and Taylors had formed Wooden Horse Investments for the joint investment in Thoroughbreds. Sally Hill had come up with the name, a reflection of the Trojan Horse of Greek mythology and Taylor's logging interests. The Hills were initially thought of as merely friends and advisors of the Taylors; the fact that they were indeed co-owners did not surface publicly until after the 1977 Kentucky Derby.

Pearson's Barn, taken from Karen Taylor's maiden name, also was the name of the West Coast stable of horses owned by the Taylors and other associates, including Karen's and Mickey's fathers, Delmar Pearson and Chet Taylor.

Horses acquired by Wooden Horse Investments, a

corporation wholly owned by the Taylors and Hills, were leased to Karen for racing purposes.

One of the first runners acquired by Wooden Horse was a 1974 yearling named Lexington Laugh, who became a stakes winner at two. The name, chosen in response to the fun the owners had had at the yearling sales, reflected their high-spirited, good-natured approach to the racing game.

In choosing a name for the $17,500 Bold Reasoning—My Charmer colt, they wanted something derived from Taylor's roots in Washington and from a swampy area or slew around Fort Myers, Florida, where Hill grew up. They rejected their tongue-twisting first choice, White Swan Slew, in favor of the more metropolitan Seattle Slew.

The Taylors and Hills came away from the 1975 yearling sales with nine horses. The five they thought most likely to win early would go to Dave Hofmans, trainer of Lexington Laugh, in California. The four others, including Seattle Slew, they figured would take more time to develop. Those would go to their East Coast trainer, thirty-four-year-old Billy Turner.

Hill, whose veterinary practice covered the New

York racetracks, had become friends with Turner and was impressed with the young trainer's work ethic and philosophy. Turner had even lived with the Hills for a time and was godfather to their son Jamie.[7]

Born in Rochester, New York, Billy Turner at age ten moved to the Delaware-Pennsylvania horse country when his father took a job with the du Pont family in Wilmington. He entered school in Unionville, Pennsylvania, where he met Winky Cocks, son of Hall of Fame steeplechase trainer Burley Cocks.

"I guess my fate was sealed," Turner said. "Burley gave me my first chance to ride a horse, my first chance to train a horse, and he encouraged me finally to go out on my own."[8]

As a 105-pound teenager, Turner saw himself becoming "the greatest jockey in the world," but visions of glory in the saddle vanished in about eighteen months, when he grew six inches en route to a height of six feet two. Turner, nevertheless, rode as a jump jockey from 1958-1962, winning the National Amateur Jockey Championship one year.

His parents insisted on college, and Turner entered pre-veterinary studies at Emory University in Atlanta, picking a school close to Cocks' Camden, South Carolina, winter training headquarters. He made the drive every weekend, galloping horses for Cocks, then in his final semester at Emory, he dropped out so he could ride one more season in the steeplechase ranks. Turner then spent five years as assistant trainer under the elder Cocks before going out on his own in 1966.

"One thing Burley nailed into my mind forever is that no matter how good a job you may have done, you can always do it better if you try harder," Turner said.[9]

The steeplechase sport has produced many trainers who achieved prominence with runners racing on the flat — that is, without jumping. The sport teaches a trainer patience. It takes time to educate a horse to hurdle brush and timber, and it takes a mature animal to handle the rigors of jump racing. It was Turner's patient handling of horses that had impressed Hill.

But the first Turner to lay hands on Seattle Slew was not the trainer, but the trainer's wife Paula, an accomplished horsewoman in her own right. Paula broke yearlings on a part of Mrs. Henry Obre's farm in Monkton, Maryland, that the Turners leased for that purpose. Seattle Slew, who had been kept at Murty

Farm in Lexington since the sale, arrived at the Obre farm in September of 1975 to begin his education to be a racehorse.[10]

"He was the toughest yearling I ever had to break in," Paula recalled. "Not tough, but stubborn. But...we finally worked things out, and he's been nothing but perfection ever since."[11]

Paula Turner gave the gangly colt the nickname Baby Huey after the overgrown duck called "The Baby Giant" in the comics. Paula, who grew up in an orphanage dreaming of horses and reading Walter Farley's *Black Stallion* sagas, had been an exercise rider and groom at tracks in Maryland and Delaware throughout her teenage years. She knew what it took to break horses. She had become adept at teaching them to accept a saddle, bit, and bridle and respond to commands made vocally and through a tug on the reins or a kick in the sides. Slew learned his lessons well, but maintained an independent, sometimes stubborn, attitude, never batting an eye when faced with obstacles other yearlings would shy away from.

"This is an unusual horse," Paula told her husband. "Very determined. I can't believe how businesslike he is."[12]

CHAPTER 2

Saratoga "Secret"

The big, mahogany colt who arrived at Billy Turner's barn at the New York track Belmont Park in January of 1976 was not the sleek racer Slew would become, but with a $17,500 yearling purchase, expectations must be modest at best. Faced with what he described as "a big, gangly, slew-footed colt," Turner figured it would take time for Seattle Slew to "come to hand" and show whatever ability he possessed.

Turner's crew immediately picked up Paula Turner's nickname, and Slew became Baby Huey at the racetrack.

"He was a big, clumsy galloping horse," Jim Hill recalled. "He would launch himself off his hind legs and land in a pile. He certainly wasn't pretty to look at on the racetrack."[1]

Turner sent the colt to the track one morning in

April for "breezing" — more than a gallop, but less demanding than a full-blown, timed workout. Turner was surprised when Slew, working in company with another horse for the first time, demonstrated that he could run a little, and more importantly, that he seemed to like it.

"It may have been Baby Huey who went to the track that morning, but it was Mighty Mouse who returned," noted writer Steve Haskin of *Daily Racing Form*.

Exercise rider Mike Kennedy had been instructed to work the colt three furlongs in about thirty-nine seconds. Instead, Slew completed the work in :35, with Kennedy unable to restrain him.

"Huey just put his head in the air," Kennedy told *The New York Times* writer Steve Cady, "and opened his mouth so wide you could have thrown a baby in there. He took hold of that bit and started running away from that older horse and I thought, 'What the hell is going on here?' "

Kennedy was no novice when it came to good horses. The thirty-eight-year-old Irishman had left school at fifteen for the life of a racetracker, and he worked for some of Europe's top trainers, both on the flat and over jumps, before immigrating to the United States in the mid-1960s. At the New York tracks, he worked as a pari-mutuel clerk in the afternoon after galloping horses in the morning. He had been on some good horses, but none like Seattle Slew.

"Just like that, he went from being a big, sloppy baby to a machine," Hill said, and Turner echoed that sentiment: "As soon as he had something to compete with, you could see the determination. He was gone."[2]

Groom John Polston, a veteran racetracker who like Turner and Kennedy had come up through the steeplechase ranks, sensed there was something special about the colt. The Belmont breeze seemed to confirm it.

Still, Turner felt the colt needed more time to grow into his big frame. For the next two months, he took it easy with Baby Huey, building the colt's strength and endurance with long gallops around the track. Serious training resumed in June, with the trainer eyeing a race in August for Slew's debut, closing day at Saratoga racecourse in Saratoga Springs, New York.

The workout regimen continued from the Horse Haven training complex at the upstate New York track, where Slew continued to wow the morning railbirds with his works, including an unpublished 1:10 1/5 for six furlongs that had everyone talking.

Turner wanted to work the colt from the gate alongside other horses that morning and needed a jockey, rather than an exercise rider, for the task. He had used Jean Cruguet in the past and spotted the Frenchman nearby when Polston brought Seattle Slew out of his stall.

"How would you like to take this colt out of the gate for me?" Turner asked. Cruguet said he would. When the jockey came back from the work, Turner recalled, "his face was lit up like a Christmas tree."[3] A partnership between horse and rider was born.

Jim Hill watched the work from the rail, along with Polston and Turner's assistant trainer, Dennis Carroll. Kennedy observed from the stands beside Cruguet's wife Denise.

Sally Hill had brought son Jamie to watch the workout, and trainer Allen Jerkens gave the youngster a ringside seat aboard a stable pony. Jerkens was unaware that Sally had an interest in one of the horses scheduled to work. Slew hesitated briefly when the gate opened, then blew by his co-workers, while Turner, aboard his stable pony Steamboat, waved his arms in a fruitless attempt to get Cruguet to slow the colt down.

"Who the hell was that?" Jerkens asked Sally Hill.

"You'll find out," Sally replied with a sly smile.[4]

Cady noted Polston's remarks as the groom gave Slew a bath after the work:

"You're not a baby any more, Huey. You're Hugo now. I'm gonna call you Hugo."

Hill called Taylor that night with the news: "Mick," he said, "we've got a colt that's something special."[5]

Workouts, however, are not races. The keyed-up young colt, perhaps needing to release some of the desire for competition burning within, slammed a hind leg into the wall of his stall one morning. Swelling ensued, and although he didn't miss a day of training, his first start was delayed until September 20 at Belmont Park.

Precisely when the injury occurred was not documented, but it might have been at feeding time. Cady, in his book on Slew, quoted Polston as saying the colt would "sometimes jump around the stall and raise

hell" when feed was being distributed.

Cady documented Slew's feeding schedule:

Breakfast, fed by the night watchman at four in the morning — two quarts of oats; Lunch, at 10 a.m. — two to three quarts of oats and a half-dozen carrots; Dinner, at 4 p.m. (except on race day) — six quarts of oats, two quarts of sweetfeed (corn, oats, and dried molasses), a half-dozen sliced carrots.

Slew received powdered vitamins or vitamin pellets with every feeding. Hay and water were available continuously, except on race day, when the hay was removed unless the horse became excessively nervous. Turner, unlike other horsemen, kept the hay on the floor of the stall rather than in an overhead rack, feeling that "a hayrack is just one more thing a horse can hurt himself fooling around with."

All in all, the 1976 Saratoga meeting was a bad one for Turner. He had no winners, and his top hopeful, three-year-old Lord Henribee, had succumbed to founder. Now Slew, who might have been the lone bright spot in an otherwise dismal summer, was on the mend.

Meanwhile, a couple of other two-year-olds named

Royal Ski and Run Dusty Run were making names for themselves on the racetrack, where it counted. Both of them, like Slew, carried Bold Ruler blood — Royal Ski being a grandson of the great sire, Run Dusty Run a great-grandson.

Royal Ski, also like Slew, was a relatively inexpensive sale yearling, having been purchased for $20,500 at the Keeneland fall sale in 1975. He had a celebrity owner, Boston Bruins star goalie Gerry Cheevers, and a young trainer, John Lenzini Jr., both of whom had a lot of confidence in their colt's ability.

Run Dusty Run, the other half of the duo that would challenge Seattle Slew for year-end championship honors, was bred and raced by Mrs. Robert Lehmann and trained by a real Kentucky hardboot, W. E. (Smiley) Adams. Mrs. Lehmann's late husband, whose big-game hunting exploits were world renowned, had founded Golden Chance Farm in Kentucky and won the Kentucky Derby with Run Dusty Run's sire, Dust Commander.

Run Dusty Run and Royal Ski, the boys of summer, were headed for a showdown in the Arlington-Washington Futurity, the top two-year-old race in the

Midwest. While those two were rounding the bases, however, the best horse of the generation was about to step up to the plate.

CHAPTER 3

Two-Year-Old Triple

T he barn area of a racetrack is a small community, but more like a neighborhood or city block than a town. Everybody pretty much knows everybody else's business, and secrets are hard to keep. And because journalists often are part of the backstretch milieu, the behind-the-scenes goings-on sometimes reach a larger audience than the trainers, grooms, riders, jockey agents, vets, track personnel, and other denizens of this ritualistic morning world.

Some of Slew's initial workouts had been credited to "Seattle Sue" because of a miscommunication with clockers, but everybody knew about the real Slew months before he made his first public appearance on a racetrack, on September 20 at Belmont Park. While Royal Ski, Run Dusty Run, and others were showing their wares at racetracks across the country, Slew was confined to his morning exhibitions. Yet, so impressive were those workouts that celebrity status accompanied the colt when he went to the starting gate for his first race.

"He was the worst-kept secret on the racetrack," said Sally Hill.[1]

Word about Slew, of course, had filtered down to Kentucky, where Paul and Christine Mallory were preparing the colt's half-brother for the Keeneland fall yearling sale at breeder Ben Castleman's White Horse Acres.

"Before Slew ever raced, everybody kept coming around wanting to see the colt," Paul Mallory recalled. "We finally found out why. Slew had had a good workout and was almost certain to win his first start, and he did, by five lengths. We sold that colt for $100,000. Castleman liked to had a fit. I did, too. He'd never had a colt sell like that before, and I'd never sold a horse for that much before."[2]

Slew would race in the name of Karen Taylor. The stable's striking black and yellow colors, or silks, were designed to make sure Slew would stand out and be easily spotted from the grandstand. The jockey's blouse was black with yellow-striped sleeves and a yellow swath high across the back, the cap yellow with a small, black, fuzzy pompon on top. The colors were similar to those worn by the great Man o' War and his Triple Crown-winning son War Admiral.

Slew was listed at odds of 10-1 in the program, and none of *Daily Racing Form*'s six handicapping experts had picked him to win the six-furlong race for two-year-old maidens (horses that had never won a race) on September 20. Nevertheless, the 18,745 fans in the Belmont crowd made Slew the nearly 3-1 favorite over eleven rivals.

Turner was a regular at Esposito's Tavern, a hangout for racetrackers across the street from the Belmont barn area, subsequently referring to the establishment as "my office." He had tipped off John Esposito, one of three brothers who ran the tavern, about Slew, and the word had filtered around. In the race, Seattle Slew took an early lead under jockey Jean Cruguet, then drew off to win in 1:10 1/5. In simpler words, nobody could touch him.

Five days later halfway across the country, Royal Ski and Run Dusty Run squared off in the Arlington-

Washington Futurity. Royal Ski, normally a come-from-behind runner, altered his style in the Futurity, engaging in a torrid pace duel with First Ambassador. Royal Ski was good enough to hang on after fractions of :22 4/5 and :45 4/5, until collared and passed by Run Dusty Run a furlong from home. Run Dusty Run won by one and three-quarters lengths, with Royal Ski second and Eagletar third.

Back in New York, Turner was following the sport's traditional path for a quality racer, choosing a seven-furlong allowance race for "non-winners of two (races)" as Slew's next start. Seattle Slew faced a better field of horses in that October 5 race, including stakes-placed Cruise On In, but that didn't matter to the betting public. He went to the post at 2-5, odds-on favorite; he would be odds-on in all but two of the remaining races in his remarkable career.

Slew's inexperience, however, surfaced at the start of the October 5 contest. When the gates opened, he seemed to be caught by surprise, and the Belmont crowd gasped as he came away last of the eight starters. He and Cruguet quickly recovered, however, and were in front before a sixteenth of a mile had been run. The crowd settled back and waited to cash its tickets. Slew won by three and a half lengths in 1:22.

Slew's first real test came eleven days later in Belmont's Champagne Stakes, a rich, one-mile race that had been a proving ground for numerous juvenile champions over the years. In those pre-Breeders' Cup days, the Champagne held pride of place as the most important race of the year for two-year-old colts.

Six days before the race, however, Slew developed what appeared to be an infection in his pasterns. He recovered quickly when treated with antibiotics and Butazolidin. (Use of phenylbutazone, an anti-inflammatory medication marketed under the trade name Butazolidin, or Bute, had resulted in Dancer's Image's being disqualified from victory in the 1968 Kentucky Derby. In Slew's time, Bute was allowed during racing at only a limited number of tracks. It later was accepted for racing universally, and along with furosemide, a.k.a. Lasix, became one of the sport's most widely used therapeutic medications.)

In the 1976 Champagne, Slew faced his most serious rivals to date. Trainer LeRoy Jolley had won the previous two juvenile championships with sons of the Bold Ruler stallion What a Pleasure — Foolish Pleasure and Honest Pleasure — and it appeared he might have a third in For The Moment. The Jolley colt came into the Champagne off a winning effort in New York's second-most-important race for the division, the Belmont Futurity, as well as a triumph in a division of the Cowdin.

Also in the field were Ali Oop, winner of the Sapling in New Jersey, and two additional New York stakes winners, Sail to Rome (winner of the other division of the Cowdin) and Turn of Coin.

But there was really only one star in this New York drama, and this time, all the *Racing Form* experts had him on top. Savvy Gotham bettors agreed, sending Slew postward at 13-10, with For The Moment the 2-1 second choice.

The Taylor colt uncorked a stupendous run that confirmed his status as the best of his generation. Leading at every call, with Cruguet merely along for the ride, Slew decimated his rivals, winning by nearly ten lengths. His fractional times were impressive — :23 2/5 for the first quarter-mile, :46 for the half-mile, 1:10

for six furlongs — and his final time was a stakes record 1:34 2/5. It was the fastest mile ever recorded by a two-year-old at Belmont.

After the race, Mickey Taylor turned to his wife and said, "If we can keep this horse in one piece, I'll never have to chop down another tree in my life."[3]

The owners immediately increased their insurance policy on the colt to $2 million, having previously raised it from $50,000 to $250,000 following his second race.

For Joe Hirsch, the dean of American Turf writers, Slew's Champagne victory provided the colt a link to a past giant: "Thirty-four years earlier, another free-running colt named Count Fleet won the Champagne with a 1:34 4/5 clocking that remained a record for two-year-olds for many years. Count Fleet, of course, went on to sweep the Triple Crown."

Seattle Slew's Champagne win likewise proved a portent of things to come, for both Mickey Taylor and all of racing. But first, the Slew Crew would bask in the glory of a championship. Seattle Slew won the Eclipse Award as champion two-year-old male of 1976, and he was the highest-weighted colt on the Experimental

Free Handicap, an annual assessment of two-year-old form compiled by The Jockey Club.

Slew was given the traditional top weight assignment of 126 pounds — the weight he would carry through much of his three-year-old season. In hindsight, of course, the figure should have been much higher. As it was, Slew was weighted only a pound above Royal Ski and Run Dusty Run.

The closeness of the Experimental ranking, as well as the Eclipse Award voting, might have had something to do with regional bias. Seattle Slew dominated in the East, the two others in the Midwest. At the time, awarding a horse a championship off only three races seemed ludicrous to some.

Secretariat had nine starts at two in 1972, when he was voted Horse of the Year as well as champion two-year-old colt.

The mighty Forego, who in 1976 won his third consecutive Horse of the Year title, had raced seven times that year before Seattle Slew made his first start. A member of the same foal crop as Secretariat (and the fourth-place finisher in Big Red's Kentucky Derby), Forego was a 1970s version of Kelso, the magnificent weight-carrying gelding who was Horse of the Year five times in the 1960s.

Both Royal Ski and Run Dusty Run raced nine times that year, both won six races, and both earned much more than did Slew, whose $94,350 seasonal total paled before Royal Ski's $309,704 and Run Dusty Run's $268,241. But while Royal Ski got the money, an erratic campaign of racing at some obscure locales may have worked against him in Eclipse Award voting. Run Dusty Run likewise finished the season in winning form, and his overall credentials made him Slew's strongest challenger for year-end honors.

Seattle Slew beat some tough rivals in the Champagne, but he never faced Run Dusty Run or Royal Ski at two. In the minds of a majority of Eclipse voters (including members of the National Turf Writers Association, *Daily Racing Form*, and the Thoroughbred Racing Associations), however, Slew's trio of victories, and the promise of more to come, settled the issue.

Hirsch, writing in the *American Racing Manual*, reported on the physical measurements of Seattle Slew as recorded by Dr. Manny Gilman of the New York Racing Association in November of 1976. Most intriguing of Dr. Gilman's findings was that at the same point in their careers, Slew was broader than Secretariat, Slew's girth measuring seventy-four and a half inches, Secretariat's seventy-four inches.

CHAPTER 4

Prepping For Roses

The Kentucky Derby is unique among North American sporting events. After all, what other individual event has at least three nicknames: the Run for the Roses, the Fastest Two Minutes in Sports, and the Mile and a Quarter Without Any Water?

The Derby is the primary goal of every racehorse breeder and owner the world over; all other major races, no matter how rich or how important, are preliminary or secondary. The Triple Crown is an afterthought; you must first win the Derby. The fact that the Derby is the most valued race in the world makes it the toughest to win. Many of the sport's most famous Thoroughbred owners have tried to win the Derby and failed. You can buy your way into the race, but not into the winner's circle.

To describe the Derby as a pressure cooker under-states the case, particularly to a trainer and owner with a legitimate contender. The better the horse, the more intense the scrutiny, as a hovering and hungry media follow the horse and its connections on an almost daily basis. Living under a microscope begins in January and doesn't let up until after the first Saturday in May.

Some handle it better than others. By all accounts, Billy Turner handled it well, despite the fact that he carried what some might consider an added burden in the form of overzealous owners.

Turner had Slew pretty much to himself at two, but when the colt turned three and was installed in Florida for winter training, the Taylors and Hills became regulars around the barn. Instead of showing up only occasionally, primarily during races, the owners were on hand virtually every morning, and sometimes returned to the barn for evening feeding. Taylor's parents joined the entourage, father Chester becoming night watchman and mother Leola taking the role of housemother and cook to the stable hands.

With a horse like Seattle Slew, the owners' interest and concern were understandable. This was the two-year-old champion and winter-book favorite for the Kentucky Derby. The alarm felt by veteran racing journalists operating under the "too many cooks" philosophy was apparently not shared by Turner. The trainer said he was undisturbed by the Taylors' and Hills' presence and that he welcomed the advice from the experienced Dr. Hill.

For Joe Hirsch, the veteran *Daily Racing Form* columnist, the scenario was unusual, to say the least. "In almost a quarter-century of covering the classics," Hirsch wrote, "the writer can't recall a situation precisely comparable to the one that existed at Churchill Downs, Pimlico, and Belmont Park during the spring of 1977. Though the owners repeatedly noted that all the decisions on training were made solely by Turner, their presence in what is always a pressure-packed period could not have added to the trainer's comfort."

While Hirsch and other members of racing's Fourth Estate expressed concerns about the goings-on around the Slew barn, a chorus of naysayers focused on Seattle Slew's record and chances for Derby glory. It took the awesome Secretariat, observed skeptics in the media and on the racetrack, to break the long-standing Bold Ruler "jinx" in one-and-a-quarter-mile races.

The taciturn Turner, meanwhile, simply went about

the business of getting the colt ready for his most serious challenge. A three-race campaign heading to the Derby was mapped out. Three races had been enough to win the juvenile championship, but would three be enough to win the Derby?

Slew shipped from New York to Florida in late December of his two-year-old season. He galloped the first month at Hialeah before resuming rigorous training in February. Again, Slew turned in a series of phenomenal works, breaking Hialeah's five-furlong track record in one of them.

His three-year-old debut was set for March 9, in a seven-furlong-allowance event at Hialeah. As Steve Cady pointed out in his book on Slew, the race would mark the colt's first public appearance in the distinctive, light brown Sure-Win headgear he would wear throughout the remainder of his racing career.

The Sure-Win extended from the top of his bridle, then wish-boned around his nose to the bit. It was designed to keep his tongue under the bit and was considered by Slew's handlers to be more effective than the traditional method of securing a horse's tongue with a strip of cloth tied under the chin.

An hour before the race, the colt flopped down in his stall and went to sleep. Concerned that Slew might be sick, Turner and Hill checked his temperature, which was normal. By race time, he was up and ready to go. And boy, did he go.

His main opponent was a crack sprinter named White Rammer, who also had not lost a race in three career starts. Fired up by the animated whipping and driving tactics of White Rammer's jockey, Slew went stride for stride with his fleet rival from the outset, through an opening quarter-mile in a rapid :22 1/5.

Slew then astonished onlookers when jockey Cruguet relaxed the reins a bit, quickly spurting out to a two-length lead while racing a half-mile in the quick time of :44. Slew didn't let up and extended his lead to four lengths after six furlongs in 1:08 (faster than the track record for the distance). Under a hand ride from Cruguet the rest of the way, Slew crossed the wire nine lengths ahead of White Rammer in track-record time of 1:20 3/5 for seven furlongs. The clocking was less than a second slower than the world record for seven furlongs.

Cruguet looked over his shoulder in amazement several times during the drive, prompting Mickey

Taylor to say, "We're going to have to get Jean a rear-view mirror for Christmas."[1]

The fantastic performance, however, sent Turner a warning signal. If Slew could not be controlled or contained, he might burn himself out as the races got longer.

"I knew after that race I had to be very careful how I handled him if he were to have any chance at the Triple Crown," said Turner.[2]

Slew's next race was Hialeah's Flamingo Stakes, then a major Derby prep, raced at one and one-eighth miles (an eighth of a mile, or one furlong, shorter than the Kentucky Derby). It was his first race around two turns, and a dozen rivals showed up to challenge him. Slew put them all away easily. After taking the lead on the first turn, Cruguet kept Slew under a tight hold through six furlongs in 1:09. The jockey let go three furlongs from home, and Slew took off like a rocket, turning a one-and-a-half-length lead into a six-length margin in a matter of seconds. With the crowd applauding wildly, Slew won by four lengths in the good time of 1:47 2/5.

"The Flamingo was like a breeze," said Taylor. "Billy told Jean that when he changes leads (shifting the front leg that hits the ground first during a gallop), ask him and see what he can do. Jean just about died when he looked back and saw the lead at the quarter pole."[3]

Cady reported that the Slew Crew had attempted to sell an interest in the horse prior to the Flamingo, but was unsuccessful. After the race, they made no further such attempts. They did raise the colt's insurance coverage from $2 million to $3.5 million, the new premiums amounting to $2,000 a week.

For his final Derby prep, Slew returned to the familiar confines of New York, albeit to an unfamiliar racing surface, Aqueduct, for the nine-furlong Wood Memorial. Turner didn't ask for speed in any of the works leading up to the race, feeling that the colt's natural speed could be called upon when needed.

Six days before the Wood, Slew worked six furlongs in a casual 1:11 3/5. Two days before, he went a half-mile in a moderate :47 3/5. Cruguet thought the colt wasn't getting enough work; Turner said he didn't want him overtrained and weary for the race and the rest of the campaign.

Carrying the Derby weight of 126 pounds for the first time and installed aS 1-10 favorite, the colt was less than brilliant in the Wood, but still overwhelmingly superior. He again led all the way, but this time seemed content with a three-and-a-quarter-length victory in 1:49 3/5, more than two seconds slower than he had run the distance in Florida.

Turner had instructed Cruguet to try and get Slew to relax in the early going of the Wood, and the colt seemed to settle down, running four furlongs in :47 4/5 and six in 1:12 1/5 before drawing off. His margin had been reduced from six lengths at the top of the stretch to three and a quarter lengths at the wire. Cruguet said Slew was a tired horse after the race. To the trainer, however, the Wood couldn't have been better, confirming that Slew could actually be rated.

Although he won all three as an odds-on favorite, Seattle Slew somehow did not do enough to disparage his doubters in his first races as a three-year-old. His fans, on the other hand, grew in number with each race, crowding the saddling paddocks at Hialeah and Aqueduct, afflicted with a contagion that became known as "Slewmania" as the season progressed.

The workmanlike Wood performance nevertheless hung like an Albatross over Seattle Slew and Turner in the two weeks leading up to the Derby. Did the Wood indicate that Slew was tailing off? How could he handle the grueling, one and a quarter miles of the Derby off such a mediocre performance?

Turner answered the questions with a sly smile. He knew the horse better than anyone else did, and he also knew his competition. Several of the other top Derby contenders had been sidelined, and Turner believed Seattle Slew didn't need any harsh racing or training to bring him up to the big race.

He also wisely wanted to keep as much in reserve as possible, correctly figuring that a Derby win would be followed by even more severe tests in the Preakness and Belmont Stakes.

Another serious question involved Cruguet. The fiery Frenchman did not possess a sterling reputation as a rider, his career until then having been a series of highs and lows. The tough-talking, hard-riding jockey had left his native France in 1965, but found the going difficult in the United States. He had won the Travers aboard C. V. Whitney's Chompion in 1968, but lost a good chance at the Triple Crown when pre-Derby favorite Hoist the Flag broke down prior to the 1971 Run for the Roses.

The following year, he missed the winning ride on San San in Europe's most important race, the Prix de l'Arc de Triomphe, after going down in a three-horse spill. Then in January of 1977, he was sidelined six weeks with a separated shoulder sustained in a spill at Calder in Florida.

Cruguet's bad luck apparently had shifted with Slew, but criticism still haunted him. During ABC's national television coverage of the Flamingo, Hall of Fame jockey Eddie Arcaro, who won Triple Crowns aboard Whirlaway and Citation and rode three other Derby winners, had accused Cruguet of moving the horse too soon.

Arcaro was not alone in questioning whether the former soldier and one-time prizefighter was capable of helping Slew become the first unbeaten Kentucky Derby winner since Majestic Prince in 1969.

"Two minutes is a long time for the Frenchman to go without making a mistake," remarked one New York trainer.

CHAPTER 5

"Goodbye, Soul Brother"

"**W**hat do I have to do to please you people?" Slew might have asked, a la Rodney Dangerfield, as the Derby neared. A mile workout in 1:41 4/5 at Churchill Downs six days prior to the race did little to calm the doubters. That was hardly a work, they charged, accusing Turner of babying the horse, trying to walk him up to the Derby.

Many felt the trainer was sending a "short horse" — one not sufficiently prepared — to the most important race of his life. Churchill Downs issued some 14,000 media credentials for the 1977 Derby, and up to fifty reporters turned out every morning to monitor the "Cinderella horse," and Turner. The trainer treated them all to the glib remarks and predictions they expected, handling the spotlight with an ease and grace surprising for a first-time trainer of a Derby favorite.

Although Turner was apparently unshaken by his detractors, his steadfast confidence ebbed during Derby Week when a severe rainstorm altered his training schedule for the colt. Veteran Derby watchers are familiar with the vagaries of Louisville weather during Derby Week, when cold, rainy days often precede Derby Day sunshine.

But this Thursday storm was different, flooding city streets, backing up sewers, and washing out any training at Churchill Downs. Having to postpone Seattle Slew's final "blow-out" (a workout designed to prepare a horse's cardiovascular system for an ensuing race) from Thursday to Friday, the day before the Derby, Turner reduced the length of the work from five furlongs to three. Slew completed the three furlongs in a crisp :34 2/5, but Turner could not help but believe the colt would have benefited more from a longer exercise.

Arcaro, who was part of the ABC broadcasting team covering the Derby, publicly expressed his doubts about Seattle Slew and Cruguet. Arcaro made it obvious that he was unimpressed with both the Derby favorite and the jockey.

That kind of talk fanned the fires among Slew's doubters. But who was going to beat him?

The road to the Derby from winter to spring often proves to be a gauntlet of survival. From nearly 28,000 foals born in 1974, only fifteen made it to the starting post on May 7, 1977. One by one, it seemed, horses that figured to give Seattle Slew a run for his money in the Derby dropped by the wayside.

Of the two colts ranked second to Seattle Slew on the Experimental Free Handicap, only Run Dusty Run was on hand for the Run for the Roses. The speedy Royal Ski, injured early in the year, came back to race only three more times before being retired to stud.

Clev Er Tell had won both the Louisiana and Arkansas Derbys, but an injury kept him from going to Churchill Downs. Cormorant had won his first three races at three in New York and New Jersey, including the one-and-one-sixteenth-mile Gotham, a prep for the Wood Memorial, leading from start to finish as the 11-10 favorite. A showdown with Slew in the Wood never materialized, however, since Cormorant also went to the sidelines with a fever.

Likewise the main West Coast contenders, who

included Visible (California's top-ranked colt on the Experimental), J. O. Tobin, and Habitony, didn't make it to the Kentucky Derby. The last-named, an Irish-bred colt who had lost his first two races at three, won the Santa Anita Derby on March 27 (the day after Slew's Flamingo) by three lengths under Bill Shoemaker.

Kentucky Derby plans were scrapped, however, after Habitony ran third in the Hollywood Derby on April 17 at Hollywood Park. The winner, Steve's Friend, returned $70.80 for a $2 win bet and would become the first Kentucky Derby starter for New York Yankees owner George Steinbrenner (whose team won the World Series that October).

The final major prep for the Kentucky Derby took place in the Blue Grass Stakes at Keeneland, Run Dusty Run's old stomping grounds. After his losses in the Louisiana Derby and a Keeneland allowance, sup-porters hoped the Golden Chance Farm colt would redeem himself in front of the home crowd. Racing over a sloppy track on April 28, Run Dusty Run came on with a late charge to get second money, finishing one and three-quarters lengths behind Gerald Robins'

For The Moment, the Jolley-trained colt Slew had destroyed in the Champagne. Jolley equipped For The Moment, a full brother to champion Honest Pleasure, with blinkers for the first time in the Blue Grass, and the colt's strong effort earned him a starting position in the Kentucky Derby. He was bet down to 7-1 by post time, one of only four horses in the race whose odds were shorter than 10-1.

The others included stablemates Run Dusty Run and Bob's Dusty, who were coupled in the wagering. Despite the Blue Grass loss, Run Dusty Run's supporters felt his gritty closing drive indicated a return to his juvenile form, and they sent him off the second choice at odds of nearly 6-1. But the overwhelming favorite, at fifty cents on the dollar, remained Seattle Slew.

With the storms behind it, Louisville played host to the 103rd Run for the Roses in nearly perfect, sixty-nine-degree weather. A crowd of 124,038, then the fourth-largest to witness a Kentucky Derby, turned out at Churchill Downs to watch history being made and to join their fellow revelers in the nation's biggest all-day party.

Slew had a peaceful morning, galloping an easy mile under Kennedy at around 6 a.m. Groom Polston gave him a bath, and hotwalker Donald Carroll led him around the shedrow for a half hour. Returned to his stall at 7:30, Slew dozed off.

The Taylors and Hills left their hotel for the racetrack at around 2 p.m.

Mickey and Butch Pearson, Karen's brother, had made arrangements for nearly 100 guests, relatives, and employees to fly to Louisville and stay in the city's elegant Galt House hotel downtown on the Ohio River.

At the track, Mickey and Jim Hill joined Turner in a bar near the stable area, sharing a drink to calm their nervousness. Slew, meanwhile, was sleeping peacefully.

At 5 p.m., the Derby starters began the trek from the barn area to the saddling paddock, giving fans their first glimpse of the horses as they were led clockwise around the clubhouse turn. Slew and his entourage walked briskly, outrider Cindy Hostettler keeping the colt away from the rail and out of the reach of overzealous fans.

As they passed under the grandstand through a

tunnel leading to the paddock, the infield band struck up the national anthem and the prancing Slew began to sweat. The enclosed paddock, surrounded by screaming fans straining against the wire screen, was too small for all the Derby runners and their attendants, and Slew's perspiration increased when he was placed inside the saddling stall. (Churchill subsequently created a spacious, outdoor saddling area under the odds-board behind the grandstand.)

Slew's people worried that the colt was "washing out," leaving his race in the steady stream of sweat pouring from his glistening body. Polston strained to hold the champion steady as Turner saddled him. As reporter Cady noted, Cruguet initially was alarmed at Slew's condition, then reassured when he realized the colt wasn't trembling, which would have indicated fear.

"Bill," Cruguet said to Turner, "I'll try to settle him down as soon as I get on him."[1]

Twenty minutes passed before Turner helped hoist Cruguet aboard, and the horse and rider joined in the single-file procession back through the tunnel and onto the racetrack. When the band began playing "My Old Kentucky Home," Slew grew more agitated, and Cruguet patted the animal's neck and began talking to him.

Turner, hoping to avoid the crowd and get a clear view of the race, sat huddled before a television set in a lounge on the ground floor of the grandstand. The second-guessing and the doubts that normally follow a race bombarded him. Had focusing on the Triple Crown — the big picture — been a mistake? Had he put enough into the colt? Was Seattle Slew ready? Was Cruguet up to the task?

There is no more exciting moment in sports than when the starting gate springs open for the Kentucky Derby, at the head of the long Churchill stretch, with the crowd roaring and the jockeys hustling their mounts into what they hope will be safe and contending positions.

When the stall doors clanged open in 1977, however, Turner and the other members of the Slew Crew had their second collective heart attack following the start of a race. In shades of Slew's second start, in October of 1976, the colt seemed to hesitate coming out of the Derby gate, then swerved to the outside. Cruguet nearly fell off.

"I remember (track announcer Chic Anderson) saying he broke poorly," Mickey Taylor recalled. "Well, he didn't break poorly. The assistant starter left his head loose and it turned to the right. He broke sideways. I yelled, 'Damn!' At that point, I wished I'd never known a thing about horse racing."[2]

Averting potential disaster, Cruguet managed to straighten the colt out, but found himself trapped between Get the Axe on the outside and Bob's Dusty on the inside. As the fifteen horses raced in front of Churchill's expansive grandstand, it appeared Seattle Slew might be boxed in throughout the race.

More than one Derby favorite has been undone by such a circumstance. Slew, however, was no ordinary Derby favorite, no ordinary horse. He knew where he ought to be, and he got there. Bullying his way forward — "like an equine Bronco Nagurski," in Hirsch's words — Slew had drawn alongside pacesetter For The Moment by the time the field passed under the finish wire the first time, to the accompanying roar of the crowd.

Slew might have gone on from that point, but Cruguet wisely took hold of the colt, content to sit outside of For The Moment through a quarter-mile in :23, a half-mile in :45 4/5, and six furlongs in 1:10 3/5. For The Moment's jockey, Angel Cordero Jr., had won the previous year's Derby on front-running Bold Forbes after a similar pace. But this pace was too much for For The Moment, who wound up finishing eighth.

Cruguet didn't let go until he and Slew turned for home, preparing for their final, decisive run down the stretch. Given a free rein and a couple of taps from Cruguet's whip, Seattle Slew responded with his now trademark burst of speed, spurting away from the field to a three-length lead. The tough Run Dusty Run mounted a stern stretch challenge, but could get no closer than one and three-quarters lengths to the champion. With the deafening noise of the Churchill crowd cheering him on, Slew completed the one and a quarter miles in 2:02 1/5.

The Slew Crew was understandably euphoric. Turner's training technique, so different from that of past Derby-winning trainers, seemed right on. For

Cruguet, winning the Derby in his third attempt sealed his status as a major-league rider. He had joined a fraternity from which he could never be disbarred, whose members included three of the riders who finished behind him this day (Shoemaker, Cordero, and Ron Turcotte, who rode Secretariat) and two others who would win later Derbys (Jorge Velasquez and Laffit Pincay Jr.).

Shoemaker, rider of fourth-place Get the Axe, said after the race: "Seattle Slew showed he was some kind of horse today. He got left at the gate, and it looked like if he hadn't found room, he would run over the top of them."

Cordero said: "We gave it a good try. When he left me, I said, 'Goodbye, soul brother.' You can't go with that horse and beat him."[3]

Turner was equally impressed with Slew.

"To get in that kind of trouble in the Derby and come through it the way he did is unheard of," said Turner.[4]

Seattle Slew was unquestionably a tired horse after the Derby. His exertions, following a missed day of training and a shortened workout, obviously had taken a toll. But for now, he was the Derby winner. Just how much the victory had cost him would be determined two weeks later in the second leg of the Triple Crown, the Preakness Stakes at Pimlico.

CHAPTER 6

An Easy Preakness

O f the three Triple Crown races, the Preakness in some respects is the least intense. There are fewer members of the press on hand — the media center consists of a tack room at the end of the Preakness barn. The horses for the most part are stalled in that barn, not spread around over several barns as they are at Churchill Downs or over several acres as they are at Belmont Park. And the infield at Pimlico on Preakness Day seems almost pastoral compared to Churchill on Derby Day, although the Baltimore race certainly attracts its share of intense partiers.

None of this means that the Preakness is an easier race than the Derby; in fact, many veteran trainers consider it the most difficult of the trio. For one thing, the Preakness, at one and three-sixteenths miles, is a sixteenth of a mile shorter than the Derby. Then there are the racetrack's notorious "tight turns," created by the narrow circumference of the oval. The distance and "tight turns" supposedly give a horse and jockey less time to free themselves from a troubled trip, although this theory has been disputed for years.

Pimlico also had a reputation as being an extra-hard racing surface. For that reason, Hill decided to race Slew on Butazolidin for the first time in the colt's career, hoping that the analgesic would negate any damage the horse might suffer to his feet. (Race day use of phenylbutazone was legal in Maryland.)

Perhaps the most dangerous aspect of the Preakness — to Derby winners — is that it often features top-drawer three-year-olds who did not run in the Derby. They are fresher horses than those who ran the one and a quarter miles at Churchill Downs.

In 1977, a pair of such horses came to Maryland to challenge Slew in the Preakness — Cormorant and J. O. Tobin. Cormorant, a son of His Majesty owned by Charles T. Berry Jr., had won the Bay Shore and Gotham Stakes at Aqueduct, then had prepped for the Preakness with a second in the mile Withers Stakes. Cormorant had the speed to challenge Slew from the start of the Preakness and confirmed it with a five-furlong work in :57 3/5 at Laurel, Pimlico's sister track in Maryland.

J. O. Tobin, a son of the 1963 Kentucky Derby runner-up Never Bend, had been shipped to England as a young horse and was that country's champion two-year-old in 1976. His European trainer, Sir Noel Murless, retired at season's end, and owner George Pope Jr. brought J. O. Tobin home and turned him over to Johnny Adams, a Hall of Fame jockey who had become a prominent trainer. J. O. Tobin had won the April 30 Coronado Handicap, a mile turf race at Hollywood Park. He bypassed the Derby (which Pope had won in 1962 with Decidedly), but was ready for the Preakness.

Seattle Slew, meanwhile, was still playing the Dangerfield act. On national television after the Kentucky Derby, Eddie Arcaro had called him "the best of an ordinary lot," and that seemed to be the general consensus.

"He's a nice colt," said Smiley Adams, Run Dusty Run's trainer, "but he won't win no Triple Crown."[1]

Turner sharpened up the colt with a seven-furlong work in 1:22 4/5 at Belmont Park the Sunday before the

Preakness. Seattle Slew handled himself well and seemed a much fitter horse than he had been going into the Derby. Still, the colt had his doubters. The Cormorant camp had T-shirts made asking "Seattle Who?"

At Pimlico, the true nature of the Hills' involvement was revealed. On the Monday morning following the Derby, Taylor had made the startling admission in a telephone conversation with Joe Hirsch. Seattle Slew, who had been racing in Karen Taylor's name and presumably was owned solely by the Taylors, was co-owned by the Hills. The Hills, in fact, owned a half-interest in all the horses racing for Wooden Horse Investments, Taylor told Hirsch.

Under the specter of hidden ownership — a serious crime in horse racing — Hill tried to explain the circumstances. He said his personal pension corporation had held an option to buy half of Wooden Horse Investments since September of 1975, shortly after Seattle Slew was purchased as a yearling at public action, but had not exercised that option.

The New York State Racing and Wagering Board didn't buy it, suspending Hill and Seattle Slew from racing for thirty days. The board was kind enough — or smart enough — to start the suspension on August 29, well past the Triple Crown.

The Derby field of fifteen was reduced to nine starters for the May 21 Preakness, with only Run Dusty Run and Sir Sir (twelfth in the Derby) returning from the Churchill classic to try Slew again.

A record crowd of 77,346 filled Old Hilltop for the 102nd running of the Preakness. Those who might have voiced doubts about Slew let their money do the real talking at the betting windows, sending the Derby winner off as the 2-5 favorite.

There were no problems at the start this time. Slew got away cleanly, and Cruguet rushed him up to join Cormorant and jockey Danny Wright on the lead. Those two quickly established a three-length lead on the field, going the first quarter-mile in :22 3/5. After the second quarter had passed, in :45 3/5, they were eight lengths in front. They had recorded some of the fastest opening fractions in Preakness history.

As the field moved into the final turn, after six furlongs in 1:09 4/5, the rapid pace began to take a toll — on Cormorant. Wright had been urging the colt for speed from the outset, while Cruguet had kept

Slew under a tight hold.

Seattle Slew, with little encouragement from Cruguet, raced to a three-length lead halfway through the final turn, having run the fastest opening mile (1:34 4/5) recorded in the classic to that time. He then simply coasted home. Iron Constitution, another horse who came into the Preakness after missing the Derby, finished one and a half lengths back in second place, with Run Dusty Run in third. Cormorant faded to finish fourth, with J. O. Tobin back in fifth.

Slew's final time of 1:54 2/5 equaled Secretariat's official clocking and was just two-fifths of a second slower than Canonero's 1971 record.

With two-thirds of racing's most demanding series behind him, Slew returned home to Belmont Park to await the final test three weeks later. Many expected that the 109th Belmont Stakes would be his by acclamation.

"It would be difficult now," wrote William C. Phillips in *Daily Racing Form*, "for anybody to damn Seattle Slew with the faint praise that he is the best of an ordinary lot. It would be even more difficult finding anybody to believe it."

CHAPTER 7

King Kong

While Slew's Preakness performance elicited few negative remarks, many so-called experts in racing still railed against his chances to complete the Triple Crown, let alone become the first undefeated Triple Crown winner.

The names of the nine horses who had won the Triple Crown prior to 1977 were as familiar to serious racing fans as their own names: Sir Barton, Gallant Fox, Omaha, War Admiral, Whirlaway, Count Fleet, Assault, Citation, and Secretariat. Perhaps equally familiar, however, were the eight horses who had won the Derby and Preakness, then failed in the Belmont: Pensive, Tim Tam, Carry Back, Northern Dancer, Kauai King, Forward Pass, Majestic Prince, and Canonero.

The one-and-a-half-mile Belmont distance — an

anachronism in modern American racing — is one thing that makes the Triple Crown so difficult. Belmont starters have never raced that far (imagine the Derby with two stretch runs) and probably never will again. That's why there are three weeks between the Preakness and Belmont, unlike the two weeks between the Derby and Preakness.

Three weeks might not seem like much, but a lot can happen in that time. In Seattle Slew's case, not all of it was good. Writer Joe McGinniss had been following Cruguet through the Derby and Preakness. In an article for *New York* magazine published prior to the Belmont Stakes, McGinniss revealed the doubts Cruguet had felt after the Wood. Cruguet told McGinniss he didn't whip the colt in the New York race because he was afraid more horses would enter the Derby if their owners and trainers knew how tired Slew had been after the nine-furlong stakes.

There were other distractions surrounding the Slew Crew. Hill's pension corporation exercised its purchase option on June 1, and the veterinarian became an official co-owner of Seattle Slew and other Wooden Horse runners.

On June 8, three days before the Belmont, Hill relinquished his veterinarian's license and was issued a temporary owner's license. It is illegal in New York, and other racing jurisdictions, for a practicing veterinarian to own racehorses.

In addition, the owners were bombarded with offers to sell the colt. A Texas oilman reportedly offered $14 million in a deal involving some property exchange, while straight cash offers of $10 million or more became almost routine. The continual response: no sale.

"We have a saying back in Washington at the winter logging camps," Taylor said. "They say when the snow gets up over three feet high, it doesn't make much difference how much more there is."[1]

In the weeks before the Belmont, the media descended on Barn 54, with TV crews and cameras tracking Turner's every move. The trainer, also under the watchful eyes of the Taylors and Hills, was determined to bring a fit horse to the Belmont. Slew had come off Pimlico's hard track a little sore, but uninjured. Turner embarked on a training regimen of long, slow gallops of up to three or four miles, trying to build the colt's endurance. Turner then "tightened the screws," in the racing vernacular, with a series of sharp workouts. He would not be accused of sending out a "short horse" this time.

On a Thursday morning nine days before the race, as a thick fog enveloped Belmont Park, Turner brought out the colt at 6:45 a.m. for a mile work, the longest of the colt's career. On the Belmont track — at one and a half miles the longest in America — mile workouts and races start on the backstretch, which on this morning was hidden behind the fog as Taylor and Hill, accompanied by Joe Hirsch, observed from the second floor of the grandstand. Disappointed that the fog had not lifted as had been forecasted, Turner nevertheless proceeded with the work. Aboard his stable pony, he led Slew and Cruguet to the mile pole (a mile from the finish) and sent them on their way, simultaneously pushing the button on his stopwatch. He then galloped back around to the clubhouse turn, so he could click the watch a second time at the finish.

"His was the only watch that caught the work," Hirsch wrote. "His trainer caught him in 1:38 2/5, quite a lively move under the circumstances."

Slew turned in two other impressive works that week, going six furlongs in 1:11 3/5 Tuesday before the race, then "blowing out" three furlongs in :35 4/5 over a sloppy track the morning before the race.

Mickey Taylor thought the Belmont would be the easiest of the three classics, and he was not alone in that assessment. Cruguet walked around the jockeys' room on Belmont Day like a member of the French aristocracy, and when someone asked him how Slew would do, the jockey replied, "Slop or mud, grease or blood, he is going to run like hell today."

"It seemed that all the past Belmont winners were close at the quarter pole," Taylor said. "So all we needed was to get there and hope his class would get him the rest of the way.

"The big thing was the rain. We never knew he was a superb mud horse. We never worked him on an off track, but he galloped on it and seemed to handle it well."[2]

At Turner's hangout, Esposito's Tavern across from the Belmont barn area, the white picket fence traditionally was painted in the colors of the Belmont winner. This year, John Esposito brought out the yellow and black paint a week before the race.

"He'll leave 'em like a freight train leaving hobos," Esposito predicted. Belmont Day was "Seattle Slew Day" in the state of Washington. Hundreds of friends, relatives, and supporters of the Taylors trekked from Washington to New York for the race. Washington Governor Dixy Lee Ray signed a proclamation, stating that "Seattle Slew's name will be etched forever among the few race horses which have won both the prestigious Kentucky Derby and Preakness Stakes...All of the people of the State of Washington wish Seattle Slew success in the Belmont Stakes."

The proclamation descended from Olympia, but it might well have come from Olympus, for the gods of racing were surely on the side of Slew and his Crew on Belmont Day. Surely Slew would have his "Day" in New York.

Although the racing surface remained muddy for the 109th Belmont Stakes, perfect Saturday weather and the prospect of a Triple Crown drew 71,026 people to Belmont Park — the second-largest crowd in race history. They sent Slew to the post at 2-5 odds.

Perhaps it was the muddy track, or the daunting prospects of completing the Triple Crown, but bettors

weren't as confident as they had been of Secretariat, a
1-10 favorite in 1973. Still, excluding Secretariat, one
had to go all the way back to Nashua in 1955 to find
shorter odds on a Belmont Stakes winner. All did not
go swimmingly on the afternoon of the race. Turner
was late getting Slew to the track when the normal
route from the Belmont stable area had to be changed
because so many cars were parked in the area.

"Slew and his entourage, which included trainer
Turner and four uniformed Pinkerton guards, had to
make several detours en route from barn to paddock,"
Hirsch noted. "They arrived some 20 minutes late,
delaying post time almost 10 minutes."

(The following week, Stewards fined Turner $200
for the delay.)

When Slew finally made it to the Belmont paddock,
the pent-up crowd let loose, cheering louder and press-
ing closer than it had in either the Derby or Preakness.
Many fans carried signs of their support, the placards
reading "Good Luck Slew" and "We Believe Seattle
Slew Can Do."

Slew became a trifle unnerved with the ovation,
sweating profusely and appearing skittish as Turner

and his assistants went about their saddling chores. Turner knew that such nervousness, coupled with the prospects of racing on a muddy, tiring track, could take a toll on the horse. Slew seemed the thorough professional, however, as he made a turn around Belmont's spacious paddock, then trotted onto the track under Cruguet. He took no notice as the band played "Sidewalks of New York." Perhaps after "My Old Kentucky Home" at Churchill Downs and "Maryland, My Maryland" at Pimlico, he had come to expect such accompaniment in post parades.

Turner and Cruguet had felt the key to the Belmont was to get Slew to relax as much as possible through the early going. But Spirit Level, whose jockey wore the Meadow Stable colors carried by Secretariat, tried to run with the champion, forcing Slew to run a little faster than the trainer or jockey would have liked.

Nevertheless, Slew led at every call in the Belmont, going the first quarter in :24 3/5, the half-mile in :48 2/5, six furlongs in 1:14, and a mile in 1:38 4/5. The fractions were well within Slew's range, and the colt seemed comfortable as he raced along, increasing the distance between himself and his rivals. Watching the race, one had little doubt that Slew would indeed become racing's tenth Triple Crown winner.

At the three-eighths pole, Cruguet lightened his hold on the reins a bit and encouraged the colt with his knees and body. Slew took the hint, drawing away. Four lengths in front at the top of the stretch, after a mile and a quarter in 2:03 4/5, Cruguet glanced behind him and knew the race was over.

Slew had handled his three stiffest challengers in rote, dismissing Spirit Level after a half-mile, Sanhedrin on the backstretch, and Run Dusty Run on the final turn with equal aplomb. Watching from the press box, Turf writer Edwin Pope hit upon the perfect New York analogy, writing that the big brown colt "shook them off like King Kong batting away airplanes."

Several yards before the wire, Cruguet stood up in his stirrups and waved to the crowd, something that was unheard of at the time. Learned racetrackers were taken aback at Cruguet's triumphant gesture, which seemed at most dangerous, or at least unwise, but it soon became standard practice among jockeys winning major events.

"I'm glad he didn't fall off," Turner said.[3]

Slew won the Belmont by four lengths from Run Dusty Run, a gallant rival who might have been a champion — and perhaps a Triple Crown winner — in any other year. He had surrendered second place to Sanhedrin early in the stretch, then showed his courage by coming on again to vanquish that rival by two lengths at the wire.

With no one capable of challenging him in the stretch, Slew coasted home in 2:29 3/5, more than five full seconds slower than Secretariat's record-breaking 2:24 in 1973, when Big Red won by thirty-one lengths. In fairness to Slew, however, it should be noted that the muddy Belmont track of 1977 had been extremely fast and hard during the 1973 Belmont meeting. Secretariat's was one of eight main track records eclipsed that summer.

"He's the greatest horse there ever was!" Karen Taylor exuberantly exclaimed after the race.[4] Even with Secretariat's dazzling Triple Crown fresh in the mind, it was impossible to argue with her on that day. Slew had worn blankets of roses, black-eyed Susans, and carnations. He had done it all, without a blemish on his record.

Fan letters began arriving by the bag full, most addressed simply "Seattle Slew, Belmont Park." In his book on Slew's Triple Crown season, Cady noted one letter in particular: Sent from a young girl in South Carolina, the letter contained a request for "pictures," a blank check, and her bank account balance, $12.80.

Shortly after the Belmont, Karen put things in perspective during an impromptu speech at the monthly dinner meeting of the Thoroughbred Club of America in Lexington, Kentucky. Some 350 Kentucky horse people, including Ben Castleman, gave her a standing ovation as she took the podium at the Springs Motel.

"I live in a mobile home, and I drive a pickup truck, but I've got a helluva horse," she said. "I think the most exciting thing about the whole experience is that we have proven anybody in America can go out and for $10,000 or $20,000 — or even $30,000 — pick out a horse that may do what Seattle Slew has done."[5]

It was the summation of one of Thoroughbred racing's central messages to those contemplating buying a racehorse: You don't have to be a king to experience

success in the Sport of Kings. Seattle Slew had become the embodiment of that message and would remain so for all time.

A Costly Trip

I t's a long descent from cloud nine to earth, and euphoria reigned among the Slew Crew, who were sought by television networks and commercial sponsors after the Belmont.

A huge crowd of journalists gathered at the Turner barn that Sunday morning, when the Slew Crew announced that the Triple Crown winner would not be syndicated for stud duty at that time. Secretariat had been syndicated as a potential stallion before he made his three-year-old debut, and his record syndication value of just under $6 million became a bargain after he won the Triple Crown.

What Seattle Slew could have commanded as a stallion at that point was conjecture, but the Slew Crew rightly figured his value could not diminish greatly, no matter what happened after the Triple

Seattle Slew, the first horse to win the Triple Crown while undefeated, was feted at Saratoga racetrack in New York with a special day named in his honor (left).

BIRTHPLACE OF
DEHERE
APR. 13, 1991

BIRTHPLACE OF
SEATTLE SLEW
FEB. 15, 1974

Bluntly described as "ugly" as a foal (below), Seattle Slew showed his strength and precociousness even as a weanling (above, left). Bred by Ben Castleman (right) at his White Horse Acres in Kentucky, Seattle Slew is still remembered at the property (above, right), now called Cobra Farm.

My Charmer (above), dam of Seattle Slew, was a favorite of Ben Castleman's. My Charmer was by Poker (right), who later became broodmare sire of 1997 Kentucky Derby winner Silver Charm. Seattle Slew was the best son of Bold Reasoning (below), a grandson of Bold Ruler.

The original "Slew Crew":
Dr. Jim and Sally Hill (above),
trainer Billy Turner (right), and
Karen and Mickey Taylor (below).

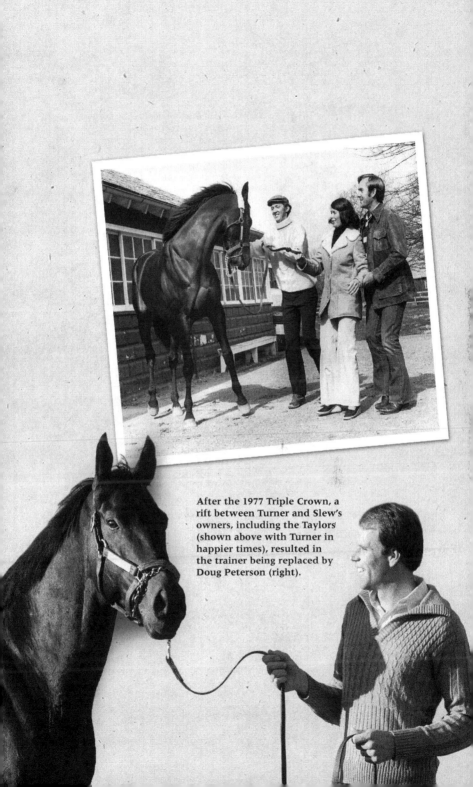

After the 1977 Triple Crown, a rift between Turner and Slew's owners, including the Taylors (shown above with Turner in happier times), resulted in the trainer being replaced by Doug Peterson (right).

French-born jockey Jean Cruguet (right) partnered Seattle Slew throughout the colt's two- and three-year-old campaigns (below). The following year, Cruguet lost the mount on Slew to charismatic rider Angel Cordero Jr. (above) after making critical remarks about the champion horse.

Seattle Slew calmly made his way to the start for the Champagne (above), the last of his three starts at two, before routing the field by nearly ten lengths (left). The victory earned Slew the juvenile championship.

Seattle Slew's preparations for the
Kentucky Derby took him from Florida,
where he captured the Flamingo (below),
to New York, for a victory in the
Wood Memorial (above).

Seattle Slew stormed to a decisive victory in the Kentucky Derby (above) and his connections got their day in the spotlight (below). Two weeks later, Slew did it again in the Preakness (left).

In the days leading up to the Preakness, Seattle Slew had his detractors (far right, facing page). But his victory in near-record time laid a lot of doubts to rest (below). With an easy triumph in the Belmont Stakes (left), Slew added his name to an elite group — Triple Crown winner.

During a tumultuous four-year-old season, including a battle with a life-threatening illness, Seattle Slew showed his vulnerability with a loss to Dr. Patches in the Paterson Handicap at Meadowlands (below). The champion rebounded in his next race, with jockey Angel Cordero Jr. aboard for the first time, to capture the Marlboro Cup at Belmont Park.

Seattle Slew followed up his Marlboro Cup win with a romp in the Woodward Stakes (below). Exceller, the Woodward runner-up, exacted revenge in the Jockey Club Gold Cup (above) with a narrow score. Slew closed out his amazing career in front of his faithful New York fans with a victory in the Stuyvesant at Aqueduct (right).

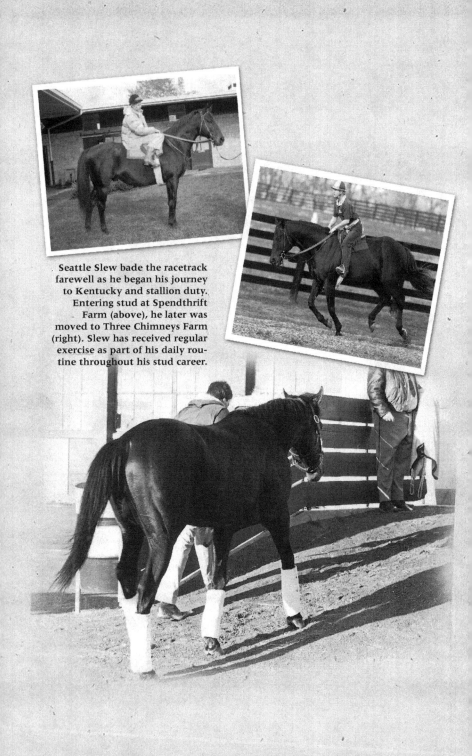

Seattle Slew bade the racetrack farewell as he began his journey to Kentucky and stallion duty. Entering stud at Spendthrift Farm (above), he later was moved to Three Chimneys Farm (right). Slew has received regular exercise as part of his daily routine throughout his stud career.

Seattle Slew has sired numerous top racehorses, including Horse of the Year A.P. Indy (above), Kentucky Derby winner Swale (right), two-time champion Slew o' Gold (below), and Surfside (bottom), a multiple grade I winner in 2000.

Seattle Slew, at age twenty-six in 2000, continued to reign supreme at Three Chimneys Farm, where he will be remembered for many years to come.

Crown. Turner, for one, felt Slew needed a rest after the Belmont.

"The Triple Crown is a grueling five weeks," he said.[1] His idea was to bring the colt back for the Travers Stakes, the famous "Midsummer Derby," in August at Saratoga. That would set him up for a meeting with Forego, whom even a Triple Crown winner probably would have to dethrone in order to claim the Horse of the Year title.

Mickey Taylor was talking about running Slew at four, something that Secretariat never did. But Slew's three-year-old season was far from over.

"Nine in, nine out," wrote Edwin Pope in the *Lexington Herald-Leader* after the Belmont. "It cannot possibly stay that way. Maybe he will take on seven-year-old Forego this summer or fall. Maybe he won't. Somebody, anyway, will get to him sooner or later."

The end of the streak came sooner than expected. In anticipation of the Triple Crown triumph, management at Hollywood Park in California made a bold announcement prior to the Belmont. The track would add $100,000 to the purse of its $200,000 Swaps Stakes if Slew won the Crown and came West for the race. The Swaps, raced at the Derby distance of one and a quarter miles, was scheduled for July 3, less than a month after the Belmont Stakes.

To come back so quickly after the one-and-a-half-mile Belmont, and to come back in a ten-furlong race, was almost unthinkable. Secretariat had returned to the races three weeks after his record-shattering Belmont, winning the Arlington Invitational in near-record time. But he had traveled from New York only as far as Chicago, and the Arlington race was contested at one and one-eighth miles.

Seattle Slew apparently had come out of the rugged Triple Crown campaign in fine fettle. His remarkable physical condition no doubt moved the Taylors and Hills toward accepting the Hollywood Park challenge. The extra purse money helped, but it was not as important to them as the opportunity to show off their champion to racegoers in California and to the Taylors' homestate fans in Washington, where Slew would make an appearance at Longacres in Seattle.

The latter was a benefit performance, with Slew to parade and gallop over the track between races.

Commemorative tickets were printed and sold, with a portion of the proceeds going to the University of Washington Medical School's cancer research center and the Washington State University veterinary school research program.

Slew arrived in California looking like a world-beater, but there was something — someone — missing. Turner did not accompany Seattle Slew to Hollywood Park, nor did he attend the colt's subsequent appearance in Seattle. It was the first public acknowledgment of a schism in the Slew Crew.

Seattle Slew, meanwhile, took to the Hollywood Park racetrack as if it were Belmont Park, breezing three furlongs in :35 2/5 the morning before the race. His outrider had a tough time reining him in after the work.

Fans jammed the Hollywood grandstand and clubhouse on July 3 — reserved seating had sold out more than a week before the race — and they made Seattle Slew the 1-5 favorite. With the souvenir sellers doing brisk business, and with actor (and eventual track board member) Cary Grant on hand to present the trophy, Hollywood seemed ready to add another jewel to the black super-horse's crown. Unfortunately, the star wasn't ready to take it.

In the Swaps, Slew carried the same 126 pounds he had toted to victory in all three classics, but this time, he was giving weight to each of his six rivals in the field. Getting six pounds from the champ was the classy J. O. Tobin, who had disappointed in the Preakness, but had prepped for the Swaps with a course record 1:47 in a nine-furlong grass race.

J. O. Tobin was fit, fresh, and fast — a lethal combination. He broke quickly from the gate in the Swaps under Bill Shoemaker and never looked back. The California-based colt flew along the California track, and the California fans responded with a wall of noise. Extending his lead through fractions of :22 2/5 for the first quarter, :45 2/5 for the half-mile, 1:09 1/5 for six furlongs, and 1:33 3/5 for the mile, J. O. Tobin turned for home a half-dozen lengths in front.

Seattle Slew was nearly forgotten as cries of "Shoe! Shoe!" accompanied the winning pair down the stretch. J. O. Tobin won by eight lengths in 1:58 3/5, only one second off the world record. J. O. Tobin's Swaps time was :03 3/5 faster than Slew's Kentucky Derby clocking.

"Tobin was backing up at the start of the Preakness," Shoemaker said. "Today, he came out of the gate like a bullet. That was the difference."[2]

Slew showed none of his true ability in the Swaps, struggling home sixteen lengths behind the winner. The unbeaten streak had ended with a dismal fourth-place finish with Slew losing to Affiliate and Text, as well as J. O. Tobin.

After the Swaps and a stopover at Longacres, Slew returned to Belmont Park. The Hollywood race had taken what little he had left after the Triple Crown and may or may not have contributed to some respiratory problems he experienced that fall. In any case, he raced no more at three.

Some members of the Slew Crew admitted they had misjudged the toll the Triple Crown had taken on the colt, Hirsch noting that Slew's "inner turmoil was outwardly masked by a calm demeanor and a bright coat." Mickey Taylor, however, blamed the loss on something else.

"I don't think we had a tired horse," he said. "I think we just shipped too early. My dad was night watchman, and he said after Slew was there three days, he was dead. He didn't act like Slew. You don't ship seven days in advance."[3]

Any defense or excuse — "it seemed like a good idea at the time" — still left a sour taste. Even if the colt's handlers can be forgiven due to their lack of experience at racing's highest level, the decision to run Seattle Slew in the Swaps was a monumental mistake. Not only did it blot an otherwise perfect record, but it kept Slew on the sidelines for the rest of the season, denying the sport what had promised to be an electrifying late summer and fall.

And finally, the Swaps escalated the quiet feud between Turner and the owners that had begun before Seattle Slew turned three. Now, with the season over, any chance of reconciliation appeared remote.

Nevertheless, Slew remained history's only undefeated Triple Crown winner, and he was rewarded at season's end with Eclipse Awards as Horse of the Year and champion three-year-old colt. That November, Hirsch again had Dr. Gilman measure the colt, who stood sixteen hands and one-quarter inch and had a girth of seventy-six inches. The Horse of the Year

measured forty-nine inches from point of shoulder to point of hip, fifty-four and a half inches from buttock to ground, and fifteen and a half inches from point of shoulder to point of shoulder.

"What does a champion look like?" Hirsch concluded in his annual assessment of the racing season published in the *American Racing Manual*. "Like Seattle Slew."

CHAPTER 9

Dark Days

W hat figured to be a bright Christmas of 1977 for the Slew Crew turned dark several weeks before the holidays. After Slew had his final breeze at Belmont Park before shipping south for the winter, Turner was informed that he was no longer the trainer of Seattle Slew.

The Taylors and Hills hired Doug Peterson, an assistant to trainer Bob Dunham, to handle their horses. Hill had become acquainted with Peterson while doing vet work for Dunham. Publicly, the breakup was explained as follows: After spending thousands of dollars on Thoroughbreds, the owners believed they deserved a trainer who worked for them exclusively. Turner, on the other hand, felt he owed a debt to certain owners who had given him a chance when he was starting out. He would not abandon them, even if it meant losing the best horse he ever had.

"I knew it was coming," Turner told Joe Hirsch. "I had some personal differences with a member of the organization three months ago, and I knew it had to come sometime, but I wish I could have continued with Slew until the end of his racing career."

But Turner had another problem that only those closest to him knew about — alcohol abuse. The hard-drinking trainer's easy-going style had seemed refreshing at first, but as the 1977 season wore on, he had become more outspoken, bitterly complaining to friends about his loss of control over Seattle Slew's handling. Many reporters, perhaps unaware of the underlying problem, tended to side with Turner.

"It was tough, but we had to do the right thing," Mickey Taylor remarked many years later. "I talked to Billy, and the change had to be made. I had spent years in a logging camp and knew what drinking could do to a man. We also had other horses in the stable to consider."[1]

"Everyone wants the golden dream to go on and on," Sally Hill told the *Racing Form*'s Steve Haskin. "We promised Billy we wouldn't make his problems public, and as a result, we took unbelievable heat. I had reporters calling me constantly telling me how ungrateful we were.

"It was a very disturbing time. My kids would read the newspapers, and it was hard for them to see their parents being slammed like that. Jim had tried to get Billy to take care of his problem for a year; he didn't, so we did what we had to do."

"Billy could do the right thing with the horse, but he just couldn't do the right thing with himself," Jim Hill said several years later. "He's a great guy and probably as good a horseman as I've ever met, and that's why it was such a heartbreaking thing for us."[2]

Turner kept his addiction hidden and continued to operate a successful stable into the early 1990s, when a series of alcohol-related illnesses forced him from the sport. He checked into a rehabilitation clinic, regained his health, and resumed his training career in Maryland. He received a lifetime achievement award from the Maryland Racing Writers Association in 1995. More recently, Turner trained the good grass filly Gaviola, a graded stakes winner in 2000.

"There's no question I understand now why they did it," Turner said humbly in 1997. "If I was in their position, I would have done the same thing. Luckily, even with my problem, I could appreciate everything that was happening with Slew. The alcohol didn't finish me off for another five or six years."[3]

The breakup wasn't the first time, nor would it be the last, that a champion has changed barns after or even during a championship season. The bottom line was that the Slew Crew had been split asunder, and what effect that would have on the colt, if any, could not be determined until he began his four-year-old campaign.

The minor respiratory ailment that had bothered the colt during the fall of 1977 had vanished by the time he shipped to Florida and took up residence in Peterson's barn at Hialeah. He trained well and appeared in top form as his four-year-old debut approached. The new Crew had selected Hialeah's opening-day Tallahassee Handicap, on January 16, as the first step in Seattle Slew's climb toward a second Horse of the Year title.

Three days before the race, however, Seattle Slew's morning routine was shattered. Exercise rider Mike Kennedy got to the barn that morning at 4:30 and took the colt's temperature, which was normal. About an hour later, Peterson arrived and had Slew tacked up for his regular morning exercise.

He gave Kennedy a leg up, helping the rider into the saddle, and put a hand on the colt's neck.

"Hey Mike, he feels warm," Peterson said.

"I just took his temperature," Kennedy responded.

Mickey Taylor showed up at that point.

"They retook his temperature, and it was 101 degrees," Taylor recalled. "A half-hour later it was 103."[4]

A fever is an alarm that usually signals an infection of some sort. Returned to his stall, Slew collapsed, covered with sweat and throwing his head about. Hurriedly dosed with antibiotics, he showed no immediate improvement.

Then another of Peterson's horses was stricken. Panic spread throughout the Hialeah backstretch. The first thought was that Colitis X, a mysterious disease known to be fatal, was the cause. If so, it was feared, Seattle Slew might be infected as well.

The $17,500 Cinderella horse, the most valuable Thoroughbred on the racetrack, had suddenly become something of a Sleeping Beauty. For days, Slew's life appeared in danger, his shining coat dulled, his bright eyes listless. His life insurance policy had been increased to $6 million, a sum nobody relished collecting.

Hill drew up a four-day treatment program for the colt after calling in another veterinarian, Ben Franklin, for consultation. Hill and Taylor spent their nights at the barn, alternately sleeping and monitoring the sick champion.

Slew's temperature was taken four times a day; his white blood cell count was determined daily at three laboratories. Slew responded slowly, but positively. Two weeks after the illness struck, he was well enough to be walked in the shedrow of his barn. When it was determined the colt was no longer in danger, the Taylors and Hills were faced with another decision. Should they embark on the recovery and rehabilitation process necessary to bring Slew back to the races, or retire him to stud? A race in Florida was out of the question, but the colt could possibly be in good enough shape to breed to some mares during the 1978 breeding season.

The owners were receiving offers daily for Slew's breeding services, one of which approached $15 million. They planned to increase his insurance coverage again, going perhaps as high as $12 million, a figure only Lloyd's of London could handle. But as the colt's condition improved, they decided to keep the colt in training.

"We based our thinking on three points," Taylor said. "The first is the welfare of the colt, who appears fully recovered from his recent illness. Second, there is still a greater desire by the public to see him in action. Third, there are our own feelings. All of us want to see him race again."[5]

In mid-February, they announced that they had accepted a syndication deal. Breeding rights for Seattle Slew were divided into forty shares, with twenty being sold for $300,000 each. That placed Slew's value as a stallion at a record $12 million (40 x $300,000), twice that of Secretariat.

The principal investors in the Slew syndicate included George A. (Joe) Layman Jr. of Yakima, Washington, who acquired twenty-five percent of the horse. Another twenty-five percent was split between Franklin Groves of Minneapolis, Minnesota, and Brownell Combs II of Spendthrift Farm in Kentucky, where Seattle Slew would stand at stud. In addition to retaining half of the shares, or fifty percent ownership of Seattle Slew as a stallion, the Taylors and Hills reserved the right to manage the colt through the remainder of his racing career.

Hill understood that for Slew to become a major stallion, the opportunities at that time would have been limited. The Thoroughbred breeding season begins in mid-February, and although it lasts until June, most of the best mares are "booked" to specific stallions well before the season begins. Even if some breeders opted out of existing contracts, it probably was already too late for Slew to get a full book of the finest mares available.

"It would have been rushing things a bit to send him to stud this year," Hill said. "He's not ready to travel yet, and there would have been a period of fertility tests."[6]

"Racing has been good to us," said Taylor. "We would like to do something good for racing."

While there was no real reason to question the sincerity of Hill's and Taylor's statements, some in the media had grown skeptical of the Slew Crew.

"Tragically, somewhere amid their television appearances and commercial spin-offs on the Slew phenomenon, the Taylors and Hills began to confuse astounding good luck with genius — and a good race-horse with a kind of wind-up toy," wrote Pete Axthelm in *Newsweek*. "Racing Slew again may be a gamble the owners have forced themselves to take. Now Slew may have to race again to rebuild his tarnished image and his price."

Slew's four-year-old campaign began in New York in a seven-furlong allowance race contested over a sloppy track at Aqueduct on May 14. A national television crew greeted Slew and his connections that gloomy afternoon. The Slew Crew was understandably nervous, none more so than Peterson, who was sending out the Triple Crown winner for the first time. Once the race got underway, the tension lifted as Slew, with Cruguet aboard, won by eight and a quarter lengths as the 1-10 favorite. His beaten rivals included 1975 champion sprinter Gallant Bob.

"He's back!" exclaimed Taylor. "All the others better look out because Seattle Slew is back."[7]

But he wasn't back for long. Several days after the

race, word came from the Slew camp that the colt had banged a hock in his stall, resulting in an injury similar to what had happened to him as a two-year-old at Saratoga. He missed the important Metropolitan Mile at Belmont Park on Memorial Day — a race the mighty Forego won twice in four tries — and was not seen under silks again until August.

Some observers, including Joe Hirsch, felt Seattle Slew could have raced before then. After the swelling in his hock subsided, he trained well for Peterson. But the Taylors and Hills, still smarting from the previous July's debacle at Hollywood Park and now with a mul-timillion-dollar property on their hands, said they were reluctant to race their charge in the midsummer heat.

Skeptics suggested that there were other reasons for the owners' hesitancy about racing the champion, say-ing they were fearful of Slew's getting beat or afraid of the added weight he might be asked to carry if he won. Some said he made the May 14 start only so the own-ers could establish him as a horse in training for tax depreciation purposes, then re-depreciate him once he had entered stud.

"No such idea has come from us or the Groveses or

Joe Layman," Taylor responded to the tax-related allegation. "I'm a CPA, and I know something about this. His residual value is so great that you can't depreciate the horse a great deal. If they dip too much, they'll end up in tax court."[8]

Taylor's maturation in the horse business was apparent as he fielded such questions through the spring and summer. He seemed more sure of himself, more confident, and more willing to concede that the Slew Crew had made some errors in judgment.

"We've made our mistakes," he admitted, "but we're young. The first time you make a mistake, you're wrong; the second time, you're stupid.

"Maybe we're too cautious with him, but it's hogwash to say he has major problems. He is fine now, and if we don't make the fall, we're going to look like complete idiots."

Even on the sidelines, Slew remained the country's top horse in training. The Horse of the Year title he had earned at three, like a heavyweight champion's belt, was his until someone took it from him. Two of the main contenders exited the racing scene during Slew's hiatus. Old rival Run Dusty Run was in fine form early

in the year, but unfortunately suffered a hairline fracture of his left cannon bone during a workout in Florida and was retired to stud.

Next to go was Forego, who for the past four years had owned the handicap division. This was at a time in racing history when champions were expected to carry huge weights. Forego won fourteen races while carrying between 130 and 137 pounds. He made his final start, the fifty-seventh of his career, in the 1978 Suburban Handicap under 132 pounds. He finished fifth in the July 4 race, and six days later, owner Martha Gerry announced that Forego was through racing. It was a sad day for the sport.

But not so sad, perhaps, for the divisional contenders who remained active, including Seattle Slew. In racing, however, walkovers are few and far between. For every contender who falls, another rises to take his place. No one was going to hand Seattle Slew the divisional title, and as for Horse of the Year, there were younger horses out there who would have a lot to say about that.

CHAPTER 10

Rejoining The Fray

N o matter how he performed at four, Slew's accomplishments at two and three were Hall of Fame material. Nevertheless, a four-year-old campaign could not be dismissed as a lark, a gamble with nothing to lose. The colt's reputation had been tarnished by the Hollywood Park loss and by his failure to make any of the big races for the older male division through the winter, spring, and summer of 1978.

The reconstituted Slew Crew did not envision a forgotten Seattle Slew slinking off to stud duty. They fervently believed their colt would finish his racing career on top...that he would again show the ability and heart that had made his name a household word in 1977. They also hoped it would be a wake-up call to breeders who might have grown complacent about Slew.

If Slew were to regain his status as top dog in the horse

world, however, he would have to do it quickly. He would have to beat the best runners in training, not only of his own generation, but of the next generation as well.

The latter was represented by Affirmed, who carried on the sport's 1970s embarrassment of riches by becoming the decade's third Triple Crown winner.

Possessed of a young, talented jockey (Steve Cauthen), a pair of attractive, erudite owners (Lou and Patrice Wolfson), and one of the sport's most colorful and successful trainers (Laz Barrera), the chestnut dethroned Seattle Slew in the hearts and minds of racing fans during the classic campaign of 1978.

That year's Saratoga meeting was a delight, with two Triple Crown winners in attendance. They did not meet on the racetrack, however, since both had different agendas. Affirmed won the August 8 Jim Dandy Stakes as a prep for the August 19 Travers and another showdown with Triple Crown runner-up Alydar. Affirmed finished first in the Midsummer Derby, but was disqualified and placed second behind Alydar for interference in the final turn.

In between those two three-year-old races, Seattle Slew came onto the track to make his first start in nearly three months. The black colt had spent time at the Spa in seasons past, but had never raced over the historic oval. He looked like the Slew of old as he pranced around the paddock before a huge crowd that August 12 afternoon.

Peterson had had a difficult time finding an allowance race for the champion. None of the other trainers at Saratoga wanted any part of Seattle Slew under allowance conditions, so every race Peterson chose wouldn't fill (draw enough entries to make it a feasible pari-mutuel contest). Recognizing Peterson's dilemma, New York Racing Association chairman Ogden Mills (Dinny) Phipps had Saratoga officials card a seven-furlong allowance race for Seattle Slew and personally made sure the competition was there.

Carrying only 119 pounds and installed a 1-10 favorite, Slew made short work of the short race, contested over a track made sloppy by overnight rain. With Cruguet keeping a tight hold on the reins throughout, Slew galloped home first by a half-dozen lengths in 1:21 3/5, just one and one-fifth seconds slower than the track record.

Next up was the September 5 Paterson Handicap on

opening night at Meadowlands racetrack in New Jersey. The race was at nine furlongs, and Slew would carry 128 pounds, his highest impost yet. Track management made the most of the champion's appearance, raising the purse of the race to $150,000 and staging a media blitz that attracted more than 32,000 fans.

It was a night to forget, at least as far as the Slew Crew was concerned. Favored at 1-5 in the field of ten, Seattle Slew went to the front at the start, setting a crisp pace while racing near the rail, where the surface was deep and tiring. After a quarter-mile in :23, a half in :46, and six furlongs in 1:09 4/5, the champ held a one and a half-length advantage over Dr. Patches, who at nearly 5-1 was the only horse in the field considered capable of an upset.

Dr. Patches, of course, wasn't in the same league as Seattle Slew, although he had come within a neck of beating Forego at level weights in June, when the great gelding was making his seasonal debut at Belmont Park. He was a son of the immortal Dr. Fager and was trained by Hall of Famer John Nerud, who also had trained Dr. Fager. More significantly, he was getting fourteen pounds from Seattle Slew.

Jockey Angel Cordero Jr. knew the Meadowlands strip and wisely kept Dr. Patches away from the rail through the early stages of the Paterson, stalking Seattle Slew. Cordero and Dr. Patches slowly cut into the champion's lead and were within a length as Slew turned into the stretch. With a furlong remaining, after a mile in 1:35, Slew clearly began to tire. Unable to maintain a straight path toward the wire, he drifted in toward the rail. Still, he gave way grudgingly, losing by only a neck to the upstart gelding. The final time for the one and one-eighth miles was 1:48.

While the Dr. Patches' camp rejoiced, the other side quietly fumed. Cruguet, perhaps frustrated at being outridden by Cordero, told New York reporters that he had lost confidence in the colt even before the Paterson. Further, Cruguet said he doubted if Slew were properly prepared for the upcoming Marlboro Cup, in which he likely would face Affirmed.

"I told those people he wasn't ready for the race (Paterson) after beating four bums going seven furlongs," Cruguet said. "I told them he wouldn't beat Dr. Patches."[1]

A year earlier, caught up in the throes of Triple Crown mania, the Taylors and Hills had either ignored

or dismissed Cruguet's comments in *New York* magazine prior to the Belmont. Cruguet and Turner had
been friends, and the champion's former conditioner
often sought and heeded the jockey's opinion on training and racing matters.

Cruguet's ties with Peterson apparently were less
binding. Figuring that the rider had lost confidence in
Seattle Slew and his connections, Peterson told Hill,
"Doc, I can't ride him again."[2]

The owners announced that Cruguet would no longer
ride Seattle Slew, then — adding insult to injury —
named Cordero as Slew's new jockey. Cruguet's temper
had finally caught up with him. The previous year, at the
height of his success, he had fired his popular agent,
Olivier Cutshaw. With Slew gone as well, Cruguet continued a sporadic riding career through the early 1990s.

Sponsored by a cigarette maker (when such was not
considered politically incorrect), the Marlboro Cup
Invitational was inaugurated in 1973 as a showcase for
Secretariat. Big Red defeated some of the leading horses in training that year (including his champion stable-
mate Riva Ridge), setting a world record at Belmont
Park of 1:45 2/5 for one and one-eighth miles on a dirt

track. After such an auspicious beginning, the Marlboro Cup assumed a place of prominence on the American racing calendar. The nationally televised event continued to draw top fields until the sponsorship ended in 1987.

The 1978 running of the $300,000 affair stands out as one of the Marlboro Cup's most significant renewals, marking the first meeting of Triple Crown winners on an American racetrack. Nearly 41,000 people showed up at Belmont Park to witness history that September 16. The other four horses completing the field were a solid bunch, but all eyes, and most of the money, were on Affirmed and Seattle Slew.

Slew's loyal New York fans this time abandoned their hero, making the new kid on the block a 1-2 favorite. Slew, sent off at 2-1, was not an odds-on favorite for the first time since he was a two-year-old. He carried 128 pounds, giving Affirmed four pounds. (The Jockey Club's scale of weights for that time of the year calls for three-year-olds to carry 121 pounds, so theoretically, Affirmed was the topweight.)

Cordero sent Slew to the front immediately upon the break and never looked back. After opening an early two-length lead, Cordero allowed the colt to relax somewhat, getting the first quarter mile in :24. But Slew wanted to run, and the pair went the next quarter a full second faster, maintaining a two-length edge over Affirmed and Steve Cauthen.

Seemingly on cruise control, Slew raced six furlongs in 1:10 1/5, then extended his lead to three lengths turning for home, racing a mile in 1:33 3/5. Cauthen rode Affirmed vigorously throughout, but the younger horse was unable to close the gap. Slew won in 1:45 4/5, only two-fifths of a second off Secretariat's record.

The New York crowd rejoiced in the return to glory of their former favorite son. The Slew Crew celebrated what clearly amounted to the justification of their decisions — hiring Peterson, keeping Slew in training at four, engaging Cordero. A third championship, and a second Horse of the Year title, now seemed more than wishful thinking.

One more hurdle remained, the one-and-a-quarter-mile Woodward Stakes, raced at Belmont two weeks after the Marlboro Cup. The Woodward's being a weight-for-age event, Slew got in with 126 pounds and faced four rivals.

Absent was Affirmed, who in the Marlboro Cup suffered his first loss in ten starts at three (not counting his disqualification in the Travers). Thinking the colt needed a short respite in a rigorous campaign, trainer Laz Barrera opted to bypass the Woodward in favor of the one-and-a-half-mile Jockey Club Gold Cup on October 14.

That was probably a wise decision, since Slew took the Woodward with the same ease he had the Marlboro Cup. Leading from start to finish, he won by four lengths in the very good time of 2:00. He did it, Joe Hirsch noted, "without drawing a deep breath."

Second was Exceller, a five-year-old owned by Nelson Bunker Hunt and trained by Charlie Whittingham, the dean of West Coast conditioners. Exceller had passed the $1-million mark in career earnings by winning the Hollywood Gold Cup in June, then had taken the prestigious Sunset Handicap on grass in July. The Sunset had been Exceller's last start prior to the Woodward, in which Seattle Slew became a millionaire. Affirmed had reached that plateau in the Preakness.

Affirmed and Exceller were set to square off in the Jockey Club Gold Cup, the final major race on the New

York calendar. The Slew Crew decided to join them.
Slew had won the Marlboro Cup and Woodward with
such ease that he appeared invincible. He never looked
better, his nearly black coat gleaming, his eyes
sparkling, his muscles rippling. He was a champion in
his prime. He wanted to run, he needed to run, he was
begging to run.

Seattle Slew came out for the sixtieth Gold Cup
against five rivals, including Exceller, Affirmed, and the
latter's pacemaker, Life's Hope. Only 25,000 fans (a
good crowd by today's standards) traversed the turn-
stiles at Belmont Park after early morning rain. Those
who stayed home ended up wishing they hadn't.

Like the Woodward a weight-for-age race, the Gold
Cup required Slew and Exceller to carry 126 pounds,
Affirmed 121. Of the two Triple Crown winners,
Seattle Slew this time was favored, at 3-5, with
Affirmed and Life's Hope coupled in the wagering at
2-1. Exceller was the 4-1 third choice.

Things went awry for stablemates Affirmed and
Life's Hope from the start. Both were lapped on Seattle
Slew, who as usual came flying from the gate, intent
once again on leading from wire to wire. But Affirmed

was right beside him, and Life's Hope was beside Affirmed. It looked like Barrera's runners were trying to wear out each other as well as Seattle Slew.

Life's Hope was not up to such a fight, but Affirmed stayed with Slew through "suicidal" fractions — :22 3/5 for the first quarter, :45 1/5 for the half, 1:09 2/5 for six furlongs. After seven furlongs, Affirmed began to drop back. Jockey Cauthen seemed to be flailing about on the horse for much of the race and appeared in danger of falling off as Affirmed rounded the club-house turn.

Cauthen later revealed that Affirmed's saddle had slipped out of position, causing the jockey to lose some control and forcing him to let Affirmed race away on his own. Cordero had a slight problem early when one of his boots slipped out of a stirrup, but that was nothing compared to what happened to Cauthen.

The tactic that was to have benefited Affirmed wound up benefiting Exceller. The one-and-one-half-mile distance of the Gold Cup was a cup of tea to a horse who had cut his teeth in England and France, and jockey Bill Shoemaker let Exceller race well behind the dueling speedsters up front. By the time

Slew reached the mile marker in 1:35 2/5, Shoe had Exceller on the move. He was still some ten lengths behind, but closing ground with every stride over the sloppy track.

Shoemaker's perfectly timed move brought Exceller on even terms with Slew at the quarter pole, two furlongs from the finish. Veteran race watchers expected the Whittingham colt to charge by and draw off to a commanding score, but Seattle Slew wasn't finished. Calling up resources no one knew he had, Slew refused to yield. Like Affirmed and Alydar in the Belmont Stakes four months earlier, Slew and Exceller raced head and head through the stretch of the Gold Cup and crossed under the wire as one.

This one was really too close to call. The photo finish camera declared Exceller the winner by a scant nose. Slew's courage and determination earned the praise of fans and racing industry professionals alike. Some even would say that Slew ran his greatest race in defeat. The Slew Crew accepted the accolades as graciously as they congratulated the winners; still, it would have been nice to have come out on top.

"Slew won everything but the money," said Taylor.[3]

Exceller won the Gold Cup in 2:27 1/5, very fast time for a mile and a half. The victory earned him a place in racing history, although he became a forgotten horse later in life. His widely publicized 1997 death in a slaughterhouse in Sweden is one of racing's saddest and most embarrassing stories.

Seattle Slew raced once more, starting in the November 11 Stuyvesant Handicap at Aqueduct. The Slew Crew had been considering the Washington, D. C., International at Laurel in Maryland as the champion's farewell appearance, but opted against it since it would require Slew to race on grass for the first time. The New York Racing Association, owner of Aqueduct, Belmont Park, and Saratoga, increased the Stuyvesant purse to $100,000 as an added incentive for Slew to finish his career before the New York faithful. New York Racing Association racing secretary Tommy Trotter assigned Slew 134 pounds for the nine-furlong race. Slew handled the highest impost of his career as if it were a feather, winning by three and a quarter lengths while giving nineteen pounds to the runner-up, Jumping Hill.

The horse who had won the two-year-old championship and had become the first unbeaten Triple

Crown winner in history, now was the best horse in training in the fall of his four-year-old season. He had won fourteen of his seventeen starts and had earned $1,208,726.

Seattle Slew won his third consecutive divisional championship in 1978, beating Exceller by a narrow margin in the Eclipse Award voting for champion older male. In another tight vote, the gold Eclipse statuette for Horse of the Year went to Affirmed. No Triple Crown winner has ever been denied racing's ultimate honor in the year of his success, but Seattle Slew in 1978 came close to doing the impossible.

CHAPTER 11

The Slews Arrive

G iven all that had gone on before, it was not surprising that controversy attended Seattle Slew's retirement. Four days after the Paterson, Louisville's *The Courier-Journal* sports editor Billy Reed reported that former trainer Billy Turner was considering filing suit to obtain a lifetime breeding right to Seattle Slew promised him by the owners.

Slew was scheduled to be bred to forty-five mares his first season at stud, accounting for the forty syndicate shares, four breeding rights to Spendthrift Farm, and one to Pearson's Barn, the Taylors' Washington-based management company. The Pearson's Barn season was the one in contention. Spendthrift president Brownell Combs II, son of farm founder Leslie Combs II and manager of the Slew syndicate, issued an angry response to Turner's threatened suit.

"If he does that, baby, I'm down on him with every-thing I've got," Reed quoted Combs. "I'll blow him out of the country. My people have millions tied up, and it's my duty to protect them. He'd have such a judgment against him, he couldn't breathe."

Turner's claim cited racing tradition. Owners of great horses routinely have awarded trainers such breeding rights. Penny Chenery did so with Lucien Laurin and Secretariat, and so did Louis and Patrice Wolfson with Laz Barrera and Affirmed. A trainer with such an agree-ment could either sell the valuable right each season the horse was at stud or breed his own mares to the stallion.

"I think he has a moral claim," acknowledged Combs, "but legally, I don't see it. There is no rule or requirement that they have to give the trainer anything other than ten percent of the purses."

Jim Hill said he could not recall promising Turner a lifetime breeding right, but said that the trainer could receive part of a season. Turner, however, was adamant.

"I never wanted to get into this," Turner told Reed. "All I wanted to do was train horses. But when I felt like they were going to turn me around like a turkey, my friends told me they wouldn't respect me if I didn't fight. Then it became a point of honor with me. One thing I can do is take a stand."

Ultimately, Turner settled for two breeding seasons to Seattle Slew, saying he had to sell one of them to pay his legal expenses over the lawsuit. He resolutely refused to discuss the rift in subsequent years, often saying that "time heals all wounds."

Seattle Slew, with the Taylors and Hills accompanying him on the flight from New York, arrived at Lexington's Blue Grass Field on a bitterly cold, late November afternoon in 1978. Kentucky Governor Julian Carroll had declared November 30 "Seattle Slew Day" in the Bluegrass.

A handful of reporters and Spendthrift Farm representatives, including Brownell Combs, applauded his arrival. Led from the plane, the colt boarded a van carrying a "Welcome Home, Champ" banner for the short ride to the farm.

Lexington Herald-Leader reporter Maryjean Wall noted Mickey Taylor's mood was wistful as he observed the proceedings.

"When he stepped off that plane, he retired and we retired," Taylor said. "We knew it had to come to an end eventually. I'm just glad he finished in one piece and retired a champion."

More banners awaited Slew when he arrived at the farm, where Governor Carroll presented Combs, an old college friend, with a plaque commemorating the champion. Yellow and black buttons were passed around to the 150 or so observers on hand for the celebration, including trainer Doug Peterson and exercise rider Mike Kennedy. After Slew was safely ensconced in his stall, the party moved inside Leslie Combs' huge white mansion.

"We'll miss him at the barn and everyday," said Karen Taylor.

The Slew Crew's understandably nostalgic emotions must have been tempered with optimism over his upcoming stud career. From a 21st Century standpoint, his racetrack earnings of $1.2 million seem almost paltry compared to the amounts earned by modern-day champions such as Cigar ($9,999,815), Holy Bull, and other multimillionaires. Back then, of course, $1.2 million was a lot of cabbage, but it was small potatoes compared to the royal sums he earned his owners and investors as a stallion.

By the time Slew walked into his stall at Spendthrift Farm, his $300,000 initial share price had nearly tripled. Before his first foals raced, the price declined somewhat, to around $500,000 a share. Once his progeny hit the racetrack and began winning important races, his value skyrocketed, with a single share selling privately for a reported $3 million in 1984. His insurable value, based on shares sold, had climbed to $120 million by 1985.

As majority owners, Hill and Taylor monitored Slew's breeding career as closely as they did his racing campaigns. They entered into foal-sharing agreements with a number of broodmare owners. They also had spent some $2.4 million on yearlings since Slew won the Triple Crown, and many of those horses were fillies and potential broodmares.

"Mick and I talked very long and hard about what to do," Hill told *Lexington Herald-Leader* business writer Virginia Anderson in 1984. "We did a lot of research and a lot of computer work to get the best broodmares to him that we could."

The owners formed Seminole Syndicate with the goal of spending $3 million to buy seven mates for

Slew. Seminole partners, in addition to the Taylors and Hills, included Delmar Pearson Sr. and Jr., Karen Taylor's father and brother. Hill and Taylor personally inspected every mare bred to Slew during the stallion's first two seasons at stud.

Spendthrift beefed up security when Seattle Slew arrived, installing a video camera in his stall that was monitored continuously. Farm personnel were ordered to check on the horse at least every half hour. The farm also built Slew his own private exercise track, which farm personnel had dubbed "Seattle Slew Downs."

Farm manager Jim Williams recalled the first time Slew was turned out in a Spendthrift paddock: "We positioned men around the paddock, because we weren't sure what the horse would do, whether he would jump the fence and keep on running, or what. But he just galloped out to the middle of the paddock, rolled in the grass, and got up and started grazing."

But Slew, who had hurt himself in his racetrack stall on more than one occasion, didn't let much time go by at Spendthrift until he found himself in a precarious position. Moved to another paddock, he again went into his rolling-on-the-ground routine. This time, however, he rolled over a bare spot and shoved his legs under the bottom rail of the paddock fence.

"You can imagine the anxiety when we looked out and saw this $12-million stallion lying on his side with all four legs under the fence," Williams recalled. "We didn't know what to do, but he allowed four of us to grab his halter and tail and pull him out. As soon as his feet were clear, he jumped to his feet.

"That was typical of how intelligent he was. Most horses would have thrashed themselves to pieces, but he came out of it without even a scratch," Williams said.[1]

Williams, a former exercise rider, also took a few turns aboard the horse at Seattle Slew Downs.

"I realized that it had been too long since I had ridden a real racehorse," the farm manager said. "Slew about dragged my guts out."

The smart horse may have been accustomed to human interaction, but like a teenage boy on his first date, he initially proved somewhat reluctant in the breeding shed. Spendthrift personnel introduced him to mares gradually or used an experienced, retired mare to get him "ready." Sometimes, he would be bred outside to escape the restrictive confines of the barn.

After his first couple of seasons at stud, though, Slew caught on, and with the occasional exception of a nervous mare being bred for the first time, he began performing his duties admirably. As he grew more confident, he even started being particular about his "dates," based on whether they were chestnuts or bays.

"One day he would have a preference for blondes, the next day for brunettes," said Williams. "He caused a lot of anguish, but all the work and sweat was worth it."[2]

Seattle Slew's first foals reached racing age in 1982. A number of them bore names reflecting their sire, breeders apparently hoping that ability could be passed on nominally as well as genetically. In a trend that continued throughout Slew's years at stud, the first crop included horses named Slew Manet, Slew o' Gold, Slewbopper, Exclusive Slew, Canadian Slew, Miss Slewfonic, Slewpy, Slick Slew, and Sweet Slew.

That crop also included Landaluce, who became her sire's first stakes winner in July of 1982 and raced well enough to earn the juvenile filly championship before her untimely death that fall. She and Slew's other two-year-olds, including grade I winner Slewpy, combined to earn nearly $700,000, more than any other stallion represented by his first crop of runners in 1982.

Slewpy, who in June 1982 became Slew's first winner, was produced from one of the mares purchased by Seminole Syndicate. He raced for yet another partnership entity created by the Taylors and Hills, Equusequity Stable, which included the Seminole partners and a half-dozen other investors.

In 1983, Slew's progeny earnings climbed to $2 million; they fell no lower than $1.4 million over the next seventeen years. His best runner that season — and one of his best ever — was Slew o' Gold, who became the second champion owned by the Taylors and Hills while racing for Equusequity Stable. Slew o' Gold was bred as a part of a foal-sharing agreement the owners had made with Claiborne Farm, whereby Claiborne sent two mares to Slew, with ownership of the subsequent foals determined by lot. The Slew Crew got first pick and Claiborne wound up with a $650,000 sale yearling. The Taylors and Hills got Slew o' Gold.

The son emulated his sire's victories in the Wood Memorial and Woodward Stakes in 1983, then avenged Slew's loss in the Jockey Club Gold Cup.

He ran fourth in the Kentucky Derby, bypassed the Preakness, then finished second in the Belmont and Travers. Also second in the Marlboro Cup, Slew o' Gold was voted champion three-year-old colt.

Slewpy that year also avenged a Slew loss, in the Paterson Handicap, and won the grade I Meadowlands Cup Handicap as well. Slew's 1983 runners also included another top two-year-old, Swale, and the sire's first major European star, Seattle Song, who won a group I event in France.

In 1984, Seattle Slew was America's leading sire, with a record $5,500,170 in progeny earnings. In keeping with the Taylors and Hills' commitment to racing, they formed the Seattle Slew Foundation which committed to selling a Slew season a year to benefit various organizations, such as the Kentucky Derby Museum, Maxwell Gluck Equine Center, and Kentucky Equine Institute.

Slew o' Gold in 1984 won both the Woodward and Jockey Club Gold Cup for a second time, and he also took the Marlboro Cup. He earned his second divisional championship while earning a single-season record $2,627,944. A huge part of that total came in a $1-million bonus Slew o' Gold earned for winning the three big fall races in New York.

Angel Cordero Jr., who had ridden Slew at four and was Slew o' Gold's regular jockey, also had a huge year in 1983, becoming the first jockey in history to ride the winners of $10 million in a single season.

Cordero continued to ride until the mid-1990s, obtaining other milestones, suffering numerous injuries, and receiving numerous awards. Elected to the Racing Hall of Fame in 1988, he tried training for a while, then became a jockeys' agent.

Slew's son Swale, who had gone to Claiborne Farm in the second year of the foal-sharing arrangement with the Taylors and Hills, brought Claiborne its first victory in the Kentucky Derby in 1984, rewarding farm president Seth Hancock for the advice he gave Ben Castleman eleven years earlier. Swale also won the Belmont Stakes, completing two-thirds of the Triple Crown, but died suddenly shortly thereafter. Swale earned a posthumous Eclipse Award as champion three-year-old colt of 1984. Ironically, the half-dozen runners who finished ahead of Swale in the Preakness included runner-up Play On, trained by Billy Turner.

Slew also was represented in 1984 by the talented filly Adored, who won grade I races on both coasts. In addition, son Seattle Song came home from France and won the Washington, D.C., International, one of the sport's most important international events.

At auction, Seattle Slew's progeny commanded the highest prices. Keeneland, which had rejected Slew himself in the summer of 1975, welcomed eleven of his yearlings into its summer sale nine years later. Those eleven young horses sold for an average price of more than $1.7 million and included the highest-priced filly ever sold in a public sale.

Consigned by Spendthrift, the filly was purchased for $3,750,000 by Sheikh Mohammed bin Rashid al Maktoum of Dubai in the United Arab Emirates. Several months earlier, the Sheikh had bought a share in Seattle Slew for $3 million.

Even Slew's unborn foals commanded respect, with a half-dozen mares in foal to the stallion selling for a total of $23.6 million at auction that year. This was at a time when the Thoroughbred bloodstock market was riding an unprecedented high. Fueled in part by the infusion of huge sums from foreign buyers, including the oil-rich Maktoum family, auction prices for horses went through the roof. In turn, stud fees and share prices rose.

As might be expected, Slew's success greatly increased the value of his dam, My Charmer. Breeder Ben Castleman sold the mare to fellow Kentucky horsemen William S. Farish and Warner L. Jones Jr. in early 1977, before Slew won the Triple Crown, for an undisclosed price that might have approached seven figures.

For her new owners, My Charmer in 1980 foaled Lomond, a son of Northern Dancer bred in partnership with W. S. Kilroy. Lomond won England's classic Two Thousand Guineas in 1983, making My Charmer the dam of two classic winners. Lomond later became a sire.

The mare's 1981 foal, Argosy, a colt by Affirmed, sold for $1.5 million at the 1982 Keeneland summer yearling sale. Argosy became a stakes winner in Ireland before going to stud.

Nijinsky II, a champion son of Northern Dancer, sired My Charmer's 1984 foal, a colt named Seattle Dancer who was owned by Farish, Jones, and Kilroy and consigned to the 1985 Keeneland summer sale. The attractive colt became the object of a fierce bidding duel between the Maktoums and an English consortium headed by bookmaking tycoon Robert Sangster. When the dust settled, Seattle Dancer had been sold for an astonishing $13.1 million, a still-standing record.

Seattle Dancer subsequently won a pair of group II races in Ireland, placed in France's important Grand Prix de Paris, and made a decent sire. Short of becoming another Seattle Slew, however, there was no way he could justify his purchase price. He became a symbol of the excesses of the industry's glory days, as his sale signaled the beginnings of an inevitable downturn in the bloodstock market.

On behalf of the partnership, Jones sold My Charmer as part of his Hermitage Farm dispersal at the 1987 Keeneland fall mixed sale. The dam of two classic winners and the world-record sale yearling was purchased for $2.6 million by aircraft magnate Allen Paulson, owner of the elaborate Brookside Farm near Versailles, Kentucky.

The eighteen-year-old mare, unfortunately, was unable to continue her outstanding produce record. My Charmer died in 1993 at Brookside due to the infirmities of old age.

A New Home

E ntering the 1985 breeding season, Slew's stud fee was set at $800,000, with no guarantee of a foal. Most stallions have a "live foal" agreement written into their breeding contracts, but those breeders booking mares to Seattle Slew thought the potential well worth the risk.

But 1985 proved to be Slew's last season at Spendthrift, which by that time was beset with financial and legal problems stemming in part from a public stock offering. In September of that year, he took up residence at Robert N. Clay's Three Chimneys Farm near Midway, Kentucky, where his son Slew o' Gold already was standing. Also making the move was leading sire Nodouble, whom the Taylors and Hills were leasing under the name Tayhill Stable and standing in Florida.

Clay, a prominent Kentucky banker and business-man who became a leader in the racing industry, established Three Chimneys in 1972. Slew o' Gold, who entered stud in 1985, was Three Chimneys' first stallion. (He subsequently sired twenty-five stakes winners, including grade I winners Dramatic Gold, Gorgeous, Thirty Six Red, Awe Inspiring, and Dr. Root.)

Three Chimneys farm manager Dan Rosenberg said that Seattle Slew, who was lightly tranquilized for the short, quiet van ride from Lexington to Midway, "walked in his stall like he was home" upon arriving at Three Chimneys.[1]

Mickey Taylor said the move "was not brought about by the impending sale of Spendthrift." But while the sale itself may not have been the final straw, Spendthrift's financial troubles certainly must have occupied the minds of syndicate members who voted out Combs Stallions, Inc. and voted in Taylor as syndicate manager of Seattle Slew.

What happened to Spendthrift could be traced in part to the ramifications of the explosion in the Thoroughbred bloodstock market in the late 1970s and early 1980s. Those who predicted the market would bottom out went unheeded, and when bust followed boom, many were stung. Spendthrift seemed an unlikely candidate for catastrophe. The grand Kentucky showplace was built by Leslie Combs II, who made an art of selling horses and practically invented the concept of syndicating stallions. Combs founded Spendthrift in 1937 and over the years bred nearly 250 stakes winners, including unbeaten Derby-Preakness winner Majestic Prince, whom he had sold as a yearling for a then-record $250,000 in 1967.

Combs also sold the first $100,000 yearling and the first $500,000 yearling, in addition to other record-priced yearlings for $510,000, $625,000, and $715,000. He was the leading consignor at the Keeneland summer sale for sixteen years. Auctioneers would not even begin selling until Combs had taken his seat down front in the Keeneland sale pavilion.

In 1947, Combs orchestrated the first modern stallion syndicate in America. In 1955, he put together the first million-dollar syndicate for champion Nashua, who became one of the long list of stallions who made names for themselves at Spendthrift.

Combs was in his mid-seventies when son Brownell

took over farm operations in 1974 as president, CEO, and general manager. Three years later, the farm was incorporated. Riding a crest of success and gambling on his father's reputation, the younger Combs added more and more stallions to the roster. He arranged the syndication of Affirmed at $400,000 per share in November of 1978, eclipsing the record he had set with Seattle Slew nine months earlier.

Other big name horses standing at Spendthrift included Slew's old rival J. O. Tobin, Kentucky Derby winner Foolish Pleasure, classics-placed Golden Act, Secretariat's Derby-Preakness runner-up Sham, and Slew's son Tsunami Slew.

But the heady ride was short-lived. The Combses decided to make the farm a public corporation, citing a concern over inheritance taxes in the event of the senior Combs' death. More likely, the move was made in the hopes of infusing some cash into the sagging operation. In March of 1984, Spendthrift became the first Thoroughbred horse farm ever listed on the American Stock Exchange.

Spendthrift, however, could not be saved. While Seattle Slew was setting the industry on fire with his runners and sale horses, the Combses announced their intention to sell the historic farm. The son discontinued his active involvement late in 1985. The father, now in his early eighties, returned briefly as chairman, but the old master was unable to reverse the downward spiral.

Leslie Combs did not live to see the end. Spendthrift filed for bankruptcy in 1989, and Combs died the following April at age eighty-eight. A group of Lexington businessmen and horsemen calling themselves Thoroughbred Stallions Inc. operated the farm until 1993, when the Metropolitan Life Insurance Company took over, in order to help satisfy a debt owned it by Thoroughbred Stallions. Metropolitan Life announced that the farm would be auctioned.

In the interim, news stories surrounding Spendthrift focused on such topics as stock manipulations, securities violations, embezzlement, lawsuits, charges and countercharges, and the arrival and departure of a string of company officers. One by one, or sometimes two by two, the big stallions departed. Affirmed in late 1986 moved to Calumet Farm, another historic Kentucky nursery destined for sale. (Affirmed ultimately wound up at Jonabell Farm.) J. O. Tobin left Spendthrift for Texas in October of 1992; Foolish Pleasure and Sham were gone two months later.

Eleven bidders registered for the Spendthrift Farm sale, conducted in the spring of 1994 under a white tent in front of the Spendthrift mansion, where the Combses had thrown welcoming parties for Seattle Slew and Affirmed. Alabama lawyer Ted Taylor placed the winning bid, purchasing the bulk of Spendthrift for $2.58 million (just over $5,200 an acre for the 496 acres).

He subsequently began to try and rebuild the farm's reputation and recapture some its extraordinary success. In the spring of 2000, however, Taylor put Spendthrift back on the market.

The Spendthrift saga made it all the way to the United States Supreme Court in 1995. Investors for years had attempted to recoup some of their losses, bringing a lawsuit in 1987 on the grounds that the farm had failed to disclose that it owed $32 million to private investors when it went public. (Private-placement investors earlier had sued and lost.)

The 1987 class-action lawsuit involved more than 2,000 investors seeking $7.8 million in damages. A federal judge in Lexington dismissed the claim, saying that the statute of limitations on such suits had expired, but the suit was re-filed after Congress passed a 1991 law leaving statute of limitations determinations up to the states. The new law was ruled unconstitutional by the same Lexington judge, whose decision the Supreme Court upheld.

Those hearty souls who had invested in the Spendthrift experiment were left with no recourse.

At Three Chimneys, Seattle Slew and other farm stallions were galloped a mile a day under tack in an effort to keep them fit.

"This is a happy, healthy horse who still knows he is the best," farm manager Dan Rosenberg said in early 1996. "He looks good, feels good, and is doing great."

Slew's stock continued to rise, both literally and figuratively, throughout the late 1980s and 1990s. In addition to those already mentioned, Slew's top runners racing in the 1980s included Capote, Breeders' Cup Juvenile winner and champion two-year-old colt in 1986; Digression, champion two-year-old colt in England in 1989; and Fast Play, a grade I-winning juvenile in 1988.

The 1980s runners also included handicap standout Slew City Slew; talented fillies Adored, Glowing Honor, and Life At the Top; stakes-winning three-year-olds Slew the Dragon and Houston; and major West Coast grass runner Tsunami Slew.

In the final year of the 1980s, Slew sired the horse many consider his best runner. A.P. Indy, foaled from a mare by Secretariat, gained the Horse of the Year title as a three-year-old in 1992, when he won the Breeders' Cup Classic, Belmont Stakes, and Santa Anita Derby. He also earned an Eclipse Award as champion three-year-old colt.

Slew in the 1990s continued to prove he could sire horses capable of sprinting or running long, winning on grass or dirt, in this country and abroad. Three of Seattle Slew's overall leading earners emerged in the 1990s while racing in Japan, where race purses are the highest in the world.

Those horses were a colt named Taiki Blizzard, with $5,523,549; a colt named Dantsu Seattle, with $3,131,318; and a filly named Hishi Natalie, who with $2,331,677 was Slew's top female earner. (His leading American earner is Slew o' Gold, with $3,533,534.)

In addition to A.P. Indy, Slew's runners in the 1990s included Event of the Year, a major winner at three and four who earned $1,095,200, and Septieme Ciel, a French group I winner who ran second in the 1990 Hollywood Derby. His daughter Seaside Attraction won the 1990 Kentucky Oaks, and daughter Lakeway in 1994 swept the principal West Coast races for three-year-old fillies (the Santa Anita and Hollywood Oaks) and won the grade I Mother Goose Stakes in New York.

Daughters Hail Atlantis and Sleep Easy also won the Santa Anita and Hollywood Oaks, respectively, in the 1990s. Slew's other standouts that decade included Jersey Derby winner Yonder and the sire's first successful steeplechaser, Yaw, a two-time winner of the New York Turf Writers Cup at Saratoga.

In 1999, Seattle Slew had two of the country's leading two-year-olds: Chief Seattle, runner-up in the Breeders' Cup Juvenile and Champagne Stakes; and Surfside, who won the Frizette Stakes in New York and Hollywood Starlet Stakes in California.

Surfside continued her winning ways into 2000, taking the Santa Anita Oaks, Las Virgenes, and Santa Ysabel Stakes at Santa Anita and increasing her earnings to $1,060,230. Also in early 2000, Seattle Slew had another grade I-winning filly in California, Honest Lady, and another stakes winner in Japan, Matikane Kinnohosi, who had earnings of $1,396,109.

Through early 2000, Slew had sired ninety-two stakes winners, thirty-five more than Secretariat, eighteen more than Affirmed, and dozens more than any other Kentucky Derby winner of the 1970s. His ninety-two stakes winners included fifty-three graded stakes winners and a half-dozen champions (Slew o' Gold, A.P. Indy, Swale, Capote, Landaluce, and Digression). He was the tenth-leading sire of Breeders' Cup earners, with $3,093,000. Overall, his runners earned more than $66 million, and his average per runner was an astounding $109,288.

Seattle Slew's lifetime Average-Earnings Index — a statistic that places a sire's progeny earnings in perspective with his contemporaries — stood at 4.30. That meant that Slew's runners, on average, earned more than four times the average earned by all runners over the years they raced.

Twenty-one breeding seasons to Seattle Slew were sold at public auction for a total of more than $5 million, averaging $250,714 a season. The single share in Slew sold publicly brought $2.4 million.

His 326 yearlings sold at auction totaled more than $135 million over the years, averaging $414,635. His sale weanlings averaged $344,422, his sale two-year-olds $268,322, and his sale broodmares $208,309. All extraordinary figures.

Seattle Slew's dominance as a stallion continued through his many sons and daughters who entered the breeding ranks. Led by A.P. Indy (sire of twenty-three stakes winners), Slew o' Gold (twenty-five stakes winners) and Capote (thirty-seven stakes winners), stallions by Seattle Slew are sought by breeders the world over. Their impact is illustrated in the following list, showing Slew's sons at stud by location and including only those stallions who won or placed in stakes races:

Arkansas — *Country Store*

Australia — *White Bridle, Yonder*

Brazil — *Tokatee, Tsunami Slew*

California — *Avenue of Flags, Compelling Sound, Corslew, General Meeting, Houston*

Louisiana — *Slew, Seattle Bound, Slewpy, Slew's Royalty, Synastry, Vernon Castle*

Canada — *Baby Slewy*

Chile — *Smooth Performance*

Dominican Republic — *Seattle Knight*

Florida — *Dr. Caton, Metfield*

France — *Septieme Ciel*

India — *Serious Spender*

Iowa — *Wild Invader*

Japan — *Slew the Dragon*

Kentucky — *A.P. Indy, Capote, Fast Play, Seattle Sleet, Seattle Song, Slew City Slew, Slew o' Gold*

Louisiana — *Nelson*

New York — *Cyrano, Williamstown*

New Zealand — *Khozaam*

Oklahoma — *Slew the Coup*

Oregon — *Gold Meridian*

Pennsylvania — *Manastash Ridge*

Texas — *Hickman Creek*

Venezuela — *Ruszhinka, Slewbop*

Virginia — *Tom Cobbley*

Washington — *Crimson Slew, Exit Poll, Taj Alriyadh*

Daughters of Seattle Slew made him North America's leading broodmare sire in 1995. Major winners produced from Slew's daughters that year included Cigar, who earned nearly $5 million in his first Horse of the Year campaign; champion two-year-old filly Golden Attraction; and Japanese champion Hishi Akebono. One of only a handful of stallions who led the broodmare sire list while still active, Seattle Slew at twenty-one was the youngest broodmare sire leader since Hoist the Flag led the list at age nineteen in 1987.

Slew repeated as leading broodmare sire in 1996, when Cigar won his second Horse of the Year title and once again earned nearly $5 million. Cigar was one of eight stakes winners produced from Slew's daughters in 1996.

Through early 2000, Seattle Slew's daughters had produced eighty-one stakes winners, including forty-six graded stakes winners and eight champions. In 1999, Slew made headlines as the broodmare sire of Lemon Drop Kid, who won the Belmont and Travers Stakes.

Slew turned twenty-six on January 1, 2000. His advertised stud fee was $150,000, still one of the highest in North America.

Not long before the start of the 2000 breeding season, Seattle Slew gave his connections a scare when he displayed some lack of coordination in his hindquarters.

Veterinarians found that he was suffering from a neurological disorder. He underwent medical treatment and resumed breeding, managing to cover twenty-seven mares, but he experienced fertility problems. A myelogram at Rood and Riddle Equine Hospital in Lexington, Kentucky was conducted on March 26 revealing a spinal cord compression due to arthritic changes.

On April 2, Slew underwent surgery to fuse two vertebrae in his neck at Rood and Riddle. A Bagby basket, made of steel mesh, was inserted around the vertebrae to stabilize the joint. The bone grows through the basket, which helps alleviate pressure on the spinal cord. Although the surgery was a success, Seattle Slew did not resume breeding during the 2000 season.

Slew had a second spinal fusion surgery in April 2002 and was moved to Hill 'n' Dale Farm in Lexington to recover. A month later, on the twenty-fifth anniversary of his Derby win, the mighty stallion died in his sleep at age twenty-eight. He is buried at Hill 'n' Dale Farm.

CHAPTER 13

"He Made Everything Good"

L ike many a divorce, it's difficult to pinpoint
exactly when the Hills and Taylors finally called
it quits. They all remained in racing, of course, still
linked by their connection to Seattle Slew and the near-
majority interest Wooden Hill Investments owned in
the profitable stallion. They still attended the sales, the
Taylors often in the company of their friend, actor
Albert Finney. Hill became a director of the Fasig-
Tipton sales company; Taylor, a director of the Grayson
Foundation equine research charity.

Their partnership had evolved into a highly diversi-
fied enterprise. Seminole Syndicate, Tayhill Stable,
Equusequity Stable, Wooden Horse Stud, Wooden
Horse Investments, Pearson's Barn — the list of Taylor-
Hill conglomerates seemed endless. They also owned or
leased numerous properties, including Slew's Nest in

Kentucky, where their mares were boarded, and Wooden Horse Stud in Florida, where their young horses were broken and trained.

They released a promotional video in 1987 in which Finney had a prominent role. The actor had leased nine mares from the Hills and Taylors and became the owner of the resulting foals, which included major stakes winner So She Sleeps.

"He is more than a horse," Karen Taylor said that year of Seattle Slew. "He is our life."[1]

"It's a full-time business for Jim and me," Mickey Taylor said, "but I doubt anyone has had more fun than we've had."

But the fun had ended by the early 1990s. There were no more laughs for the pair of couples, especially not in Lexington, where Hill filed suit against his former partner in June of 1992, charging that Taylor mismanaged the assets of Wooden Horse Investments. Hill claimed Taylor "siphoned off" Wooden Horse money into the Washington-based Pearson's Barn management company, which managed the racing and breeding stock owned by Wooden Horse.

Hill also accused Taylor of using partnership funds to

purchase gifts and improperly compensate family members and relatives.

That fall, Wooden Horse sold its forty-six percent interest in Wooden Horse Stud in Florida to Allen Paulson (owner of Cigar). The following summer, the beginning of the dispersal of Wooden Horse holdings started with the auction of the Wooden Horse yearlings at the Keeneland summer sale, where five horses were sold for a total of $835,000. The dispersal, it was noted, would not affect the seventeen Seattle Slew shares owned by Wooden Horse.

A jury trial into the dispute began in Lexington federal court in November of 1993. With the trial under way, the Taylors and Hills sold the Wooden Horse breeding stock at the Keeneland November sale. The twenty-three Wooden Horse animals brought a total of $3,976,500. Wooden Horse and other partners sold two horses for $520,000, and the Taylors sold three for $899,000.

The trial lasted less than a month. Siding with Hill, the jury awarded the Florida veterinarian $4.4 million. The Slew Crew's great adventure — often exhilarating, sometimes harrowing, but never dull — had ended.

"People do get divorced," said Sally Hill in 1997. "It certainly wasn't what any of us wanted as the outcome. We still speak to each other at the sales.

"Even with all the controversies," she added, "I still thank God for all the wonderful memories. No one can take that away from us. Even today, when I feel under the gun or depressed, I pop in a tape and watch one of Slew's races. All I can think of is what an incredible story it was and how lucky we were to be part of it."[2]

Most of the people who came in contact with Slew probably felt the same way, those individuals ranging from Queen Elizabeth II, who visited the horse at Three Chimneys, to Tom Wade, who became Slew's groom at Spendthrift and moved with the stallion to Three Chimneys.

In 1999, Wade and Slew (and the sport of racing) received some national publicity when Land's End Direct Merchants featured a story on the horse and groom in its March clothing catalog. Joe McNally's remarkable cover photograph shows only the left side of the horse's face, its bone structure creating curves and shadows that seem carved from some dark chocolate stone. The gray stubble along his jowl and his white eyelashes suggest age, but his skin shimmers and his eye — a fluid, amber jewel — is the eye of youth.

The Land's End story, written by David Dorsey and titled "It's About Heart," details the seventeen-year relationship between horse and handler. He describes a morning at Three Chimneys:

"It's the sort of morning horses love, brisk and fragrant. Tom lets Slew out for his ride. Afterward, he brushes Slew. Feeds him. Takes his temperature. Sprays him with a hose and squeegees off the water.

"Occasionally, Tom talks to him: 'Hey? Life is good, isn't it? Could be better if we had a mare.' He doesn't whisper. He talks, one friend to another. Now and then, Tom raises his voice. Slew doesn't ignore it."

Dorsey noted that Slew occasionally expressed his own temper over the years, having bitten Wade five times on the chest.

"It's your own karma coming back at you," Wade told Dorsey. "It's Slew's way of saying, 'If you don't handle me properly, you don't clean my stall, you don't feed me, if you bad-mouth me, I'll bite you. I'll make you pay.'

"I've taught that horse nothing. He's taught me

everything I know. His teeth will show you the way."

You hear it each time a horse wins a big race: "He's the best of a bad lot." Such criticism stalked Seattle Slew throughout his two- and three-year-old seasons. It might be hard to believe now that Slew's two-year-old championship was debated at the time or that his Horse of the Year title at three stirred controversy.

Slew silenced his critics time and again. Had he never gone to stud, he still would rank among the great Thoroughbreds of all time; he was elected to the Racing Hall of Fame in 1981, a year before his first foals raced. In the breeding shed, he became one of the most influential Thoroughbreds of all time. Champion runners who become leading sires are not exactly a rarity in the sport, but seldom do they achieve Slew's level of success in both endeavors.

Bloodlines alone cannot account for a particular horse's superiority, both on the racetrack and in the breeding shed. It seemed almost certain in the 1970s that Secretariat would be the horse to carry on the Bold Ruler lineage; instead, it was Seattle Slew and his sons and daughters who kept the venerable line viable.

Slew's impact, however, extends beyond racing

industry facts and figures. How many new owners buy horses even today with the knowledge that a single animal created an empire? How many youngsters of the late 1970s had their thoughts — and lives — turned to racing by the magic of Seattle Slew?

Remember those photos Christine Mallory took of Seattle Slew as a foal at breeder Ben Castleman's White Horse Acres farm? They became collectors' items. Inundated by requests from around the world, Christine quickly ran out of the 500 copies she had made. One set went to President Jimmy Carter's daughter Amy, who hung them in her room at the White House. Castleman, who retired from the restaurant business during Slew's three-year-old season, remained active in the sport as a breeder and member of the Kentucky Racing Commission. After his death in 1983, White Horse Acres became part of Robert Brennan's Due Process Farm until 1995, when it was purchased by Gary and Betty Biszantz and renamed Cobra Farm.

In March of 1999, a daughter of Seattle Slew was foaled in the same stall where My Charmer gave birth to the champion twenty-five years earlier.

"We'll definitely keep this filly and race her," said Cobra farm manager Jeanne Cox-Owens. "We hope she carries on the tradition of her father and becomes a great runner. One day, she'll be a member of our broodmare band."[3]

Seattle Slew touched many lives, from Queens and First Daughters to grooms and racing fans. And no matter how remote the association, how tenuous the connection, all were uplifted.

Mickey Taylor, speaking to *The Blood-Horse* from his home in Sun Valley, Idaho, in a 1997 interview, perhaps summed it up best. "He made good owners, good trainers, and good jockeys," Taylor said. "He made everything good."

SEATTLE SLEW

EPILOGUE

Measuring Up

The 1970s was a tumultuous decade in America. Its watch words included Watergate, the Equal Rights Amendment, "All in the Family," "Roots," school busing, trade with Communist China, Disney World, George Wallace, Bobby Fischer, Roe vs. Wade, Saigon, Jimmy Hoffa, the death penalty, Love Canal, Three Mile Island, Star Wars, and VCRs.

In Thoroughbred racing, the 1970s has been called "The Decade of Champions." There were three Triple Crown winners — Secretariat, Seattle Slew, and Affirmed — and scores of other magnificent racers. The list includes Forego, John Henry, Alydar, Spectacular Bid, Ruffian, Shuvee, Dahlia, Cougar, Ack Ack, and Susan's Girl, plus European stars Nijinsky II, Roberto, Mill Reef, Allez France, and Troy, and Kingsclere in Australia.

The Triple Crown winners of the 1970s came three decades after the Triple Crown winners of the 1940s (Whirlaway, Count Fleet, Assault, and Citation). In the 1950s and 1960s, the Triple Crown had begun to seem like an impossible dream.

As the decades have passed, there has been talk in racing circles of altering the series — putting more time between the races or shortening the distance of the Belmont Stakes. With or without changes, it was not inconceivable that the 2000s would produce another Triple Crown winner, or two, or three. Sure enough, American Pharoah won the Triple Crown in 2015. And then, in 2018, Justify joined Seattle Slew in history, becoming the second horse to capture the Triple Crown undefeated.

Yet if other horses emerge who have the strength, courage, and stamina to conquer the sport's supreme challenge, they will have to do even more, much more, to stand alongside a horse called Slew.

SEATTLE SLEW's
PEDIGREE

		Bold Ruler, 1954	**Nasrullah** Miss Disco
	Boldnesian, 1963		
		Alanesian, 1954	Polynesian Alablue
BOLD REASONING, dkb/br, 1968			
		Hail to Reason, 1958	Turn-to Nothirdchance
	Reason to Earn, 1963		
SEATTLE SLEW, **dark bay or brown,** **February 15, 1974**		Sailing Home, 1948	Wait A Bit Marching Home
		Round Table, 1954	Princequillo Knight's Daughter
	Poker, 1963		
		Glamour, 1953	**Nasrullah** Striking
MY CHARMER, b, 1969			
		Jet Action, 1951	Jet Pilot Blusher
	Fair Charmer, 1959		
		Myrtle Charm, 1946	Alsab Crepe Myrtle

152

SEATTLE SLEW's RACE RECORD

Seattle Slew — dkbbr. c. 1974, by Bold Reasoning (Boldnesian)–My Charmer, by Poker — **Lifetime record: 17 14 2 0 $1,208,726**

Own.– Tayhill Stable
Br.– B.S. Castleman (Ky)
Tr.– Douglas Peterson

11Nov78- 8Aqu	fst 1⅛	:46^4 1:10 1:34^2 1:47^2	3↑ Stuyvesant H-G3	1	1	1½	1^3	1^3	1¾	Cordero A Jr	134	*.10	98-12	SeattleSlew134¾JumpingHill115^{2}¾WisePhlp113½	Ridden out	5
14Oct78- 8Bel	sly 1½	:45^1 1:09^2 2:01^4 2:27^1	3↑ J C Gold Cup-G1	1	1	1^{hd}	1^{hd}	2½	2no	Cordero A Jr	126	*.60	84-13	Exceller126^{no}SeattleSlew126^{14}GrtContrctor126^{4}¾	Bore out	6
30Sep78- 8Bel	fst 1¼	:47^3 1:10^4 1:35^1 2:00	3↑ Woodward-G1	5	1	1^2	12½	12½	1^4	Cordero A Jr	126	*.30	109-12	SeattleSlew126^{4}Exceller126^{6}¾It'sFreezng126^{no}	Ridden out	5
16Sep78- 8Bel	fst 1⅛	:47 1:10^1 1:33^3 1:45^4	3↑ Marlboro Cup H-G1	4	1	12½	12½	1^3	1^3	Cordero A Jr	128	2.10	98-12	Seattle Slew128^{3}Affirmed124^{5}Nasty and Bold118^4	Driving	6
	Previously owned by Karen L. Taylor															
5Sep78- 6Med	fst 1⅛	:46 1:09^4 1:35 1:48	3↑ Paterson H-G3	10	1	13½	11½	1½	2^{nk}	Cruguet J	128	*.20	93-13	Dr.Patches114^{nk}SeattleSlew128¼It'sFrzng112^5	Drifted in	10
12Aug78- 7Sar	sly 7f	:22 :44^4 1:09^1 1:21^3	3↑ Alw 25000	5	2	1^1	1^5	1^4	1^6	Cruguet J	119	*.10	97-18	SeattleSlew119^{6}ProudBirdie115^{2}¾CapitalIdea115^{16}	Handily	5
14May78- 7Aqu	sly 7f	:22^4 :45^3 1:10^1 1:22^4	4↑ Alw 25000	3	3	2½	11½	1^7	18¼	Cruguet J	122	*.10	87-26	SeattleSlew122^{8}¼ProudArion119^{1}¼Capult'sSong115^5	Handily	6
	Previously trained by William Turner Jr															
3Jly77- 8Hol	fst 1¼	:45^2 1:09^1 1:33^3 1:58^3	Swaps-G1	2	2	3^2	3^6	4^{11}	4^{16}	Cruguet J	126	*.20	82-11	J.O. Tobin120^{8}Affiliate117^{no}Text120^8	Steadied,bore in	7
11Jun77- 8Bel	my 1½	:48^2 1:14 2:03^4 2:29^3	Belmont-G1	5	1	1½	1^4	13½	1^4	Cruguet J	126	*.40	72-17	SeattleSlw126^{4}RunDstyRun126^{2}Sanhedrn126^{2}¼	Handy score	8
21May77- 8Pim	fst 1$\frac{3}{16}$	:45^3 1:09^4 1:34^4 1:54^2	Preakness-G1	8	2	1^{hd}	2½	1^3	11½	Cruguet J	126	*.40	98-10	Seattle Slew126^{1}½Iron Constitution126^{2}Run Dusty Run126^{1}¼		9
	Drew clear															
7May77- 8CD	fst 1¼	:45^4 1:10^3 1:36 2:02^1	Ky Derby-G1	4	2	2^{hd}	1^{hd}	1^3	11¾	Cruguet J	126	*.50	86-12	SeattleSlew126^{1}¾RunDstyRn126^{nk}Sanhdrn126^{3}¼	Ridden out	15
23Apr77- 8Aqu	fst 1⅛	:47^4 1:12^1 1:36^3 1:49^3	Wood Memorial-G1	6	1	1^{hd}	11½	1^6	13¼	Cruguet J	126	*.10	87-13	Seattle Slew126^{3}¼Sanhedrin126^{4}½Catalan126^{hd}	Handily	7
26Mar77- 9Hia	fst 1⅛	:45^1 1:09 1:34 1:47^2	Flamingo-G1	4	1	11½	1^6	1^6	1^4	Cruguet J	122	*.20	95-15	SeattleSlew122^{4}Gboul122^{nk}FortPrvl122^{4}½	Speed in reserve	13
9Mar77- 9Hia	fst 7f	:22^1 :44 1:08 1:20^3	Alw 7000	2	6	1^{hd}	1^2	1^4	1^9	Cruguet J	117	*.10	102-10	SeattleSlw117^{9}WhitRammr122^{3}½SmashingNatv119^{2}½	Easily	8
16Oct76- 8Bel	fst 1	:23^2 :46 1:10 1:34^2	Champagne-G1	3	1	1^2	1^2	1^3	19¾	Cruguet J	122	*1.30	96-13	SeattleSlw122^{9}¾FortheMoment122^{1}¼SltoRom122^3	Easy score	10
5Oct76- 7Bel	fst 7f	:22^3 :45^4 1:09^2 1:22	Alw 11000	1	8	11½	1^1	1^3	13½	Cruguet J	122	*.40	92-13	SeattleSlew122^{3}½CruiseonIn119^{6}Lancer'sPrid117^{2}¼	Handily	8
20Sep76- 5Bel	fst 6f	:22^2 :45^2 1:10^1	Md Sp Wt	8	10	1½	1^2	1^5	1^5	Cruguet J	122	*2.60	91-12	Seattle Slew122^{5}Proud Arion122½Prince Andrew122^2	Easily	12

Copyrighted © 2000 by Daily Racing Form, Inc. Reprinted from the book "Champions" (DRF Press)

Index

References

Chapter 1
1. Herbert, Kimberly S. "A Fairy Tale Come True," *The Blood-Horse*, April 30, 1994, p. 2126-7.
2. Ibid.
3. Cady, Steve. *Seattle Slew*. (New York: The Viking Press, 1977). p. 24.
4. Schmitz, David. "He Made Everything Good," *The Blood-Horse*, April 26, 1997, p. 2388-92.
5. Haskin, Steve. "Seattle Slew Donned 1977's Crown," *Daily Racing Form*, April 26, 1997.
6. Ibid.
7. Ibid.
8. *The Backstretch*, July, 1977, p. 11-18.
9. Ibid.
10. Cady, p. 41.
11. *The Backstretch*, July, 1977.
12. Cady, p. 46.

Chapter 2
1. Haskin, "Seattle Slew Donned 1977's Crown."
2. Ibid.
3. *The Backstretch*, July, 1977.
4. Haskin, "Seattle Slew Donned 1977's Crown."
5. Cady, p. 12.

Chapter 3
1. Haskin, "Seattle Slew Donned 1977's Crown."
2. Herbert, "A Fairy Tale Come True."
3. Haskin, "Seattle Slew Donned 1977's Crown."

Chapter 4
1. Cady, p. 82.
2. Haskin, "Seattle Slew Donned 1977's Crown."
3. Schmitz, "He Made Everything Good."

Chapter 5
1. Cady, p. 93.
2. Schmitz, "He Made Everything Good."
3. Farrington, Merry. "Seattle Slew: National Superstar, Northwest Hero," *The Washington Horse*, June, 1977, p. 964-7.
4. Haskin, "Seattle Slew Donned 1977's Crown."

Chapter 6
1. Cady, p. 104.

Chapter 7

1. *The Backstretch*, July, 1977.
2. Schmitz, "He Made Everything Good."
3. Joyce, Dick. "Champion to Receive Long Rest," *Lexington Herald-Leader*, June 12, 1977.
4. Pope, Edwin. "Slew Did It In Spades," *Lexington Herald-Leader*, June 12, 1977.
5. *The Backstretch*, July, 1977.

Chapter 8

1. Joyce, Dick. "Champion to Receive Long Rest."
2. Hirsch, Joe. "1977 Racing in Review," *American Racing Manual*. (Daily Racing Form, Inc., 1978).
3. Schmitz, "He Made Everything Good."

Chapter 9

1. Schmitz, "He Made Everything Good."
2. Haskin, "Seattle Slew Donned 1977's Crown."
3. Ibid.
4. Schmitz, "He Made Everything Good."
5. Hirsch, Joe. Daily Racing Form, February 2, 1978.
6. Ibid.
7. Reed, Billy. "Happy Days Are Here Again for Slew, Owners," *Louisville Courier-Journal*, May 15, 1978.
8. Rudy, William H. "Status of Slew," *The Blood-Horse*, June 12, 1978.

Chapter 10

1. Haskin, "Seattle Slew Donned 1977's Crown."
2. Ibid.
3. Hirsch, Joe. "1978 Racing in Review," *American Racing Manual*. (Daily Racing Form, Inc., 1979).

Chapter 11

1. Chamblin, Keith. "More Than A Horse," *The Blood-Horse*, April 18, 1987.
2. Ibid.

Chapter 12

1. Herbert, Kimberly S. "Slew Moved," *The Blood-Horse*, September 14, 1985.

Chapter 13

1. Chamblin, Keith. "More Than A Horse."
2. Haskin, "Seattle Slew Donned 1977's Crown."
3. Biles, Deirdre B. "Slew of Memories," *The Blood-Horse*, March 20, 1999.

Photo Credits

Cover photo: (Jerry Frutkoff/James McCue)

Page 1: "Seattle Slew Day" (Bob Coglianese); Seattle Slew head shot (Anne M. Eberhardt)

Page 2: Seattle Slew as a foal (Christine Mallory); as a suckling (Tony Leonard); "birthplace" plaque (Anne M. Eberhardt); Ben Castleman (The Blood-Horse)

Page 3: Bold Reasoning (Jim Raftery); My Charmer (Tony Leonard); Poker (Turfotos)

Page 4: Billy Turner, Dr. Jim and Sally Hill (Barbara D. Livingston); Karen and Mickey Taylor (Four Footed Fotos)

Page 5: Seattle Slew with Turner and Taylors (The Blood-Horse); Slew with Doug Peterson (New York Racing Association)

Page 6: Jean Cruguet aboard Slew and watching workouts (The Blood-Horse); Angel Cordero Jr. (Barbara D. Livingston)

Page 7: Seattle Slew in Champagne post parade and winning the Champagne (New York Racing Association)

Page 8: Seattle Slew winning the Flamingo (Tim Chapman); Winning the Wood Memorial (New York Racing Association)

Page 9: Seattle Slew winning the Kentucky Derby (Lexington Herald-Leader); Derby Trophy presentation (The Blood-Horse); Preakness winner's circle (Jerry Frutkoff/James McCue)

Page 10-11: "Seattle Who?" (The Blood-Horse); Winning the Preakness (Jerry Frutkoff/James McCue); Winning the Belmont (Richard Drew/AP); Triple Crown blanket (New York Racing Association)

Page 12: Dr. Patches winning the Paterson (Jim Raftery); Marlboro Cup winner's circle (Bob Coglianese)

Page 13: Seattle Slew winning the Woodward, Exceller winning the Jockey Club Gold Cup, Slew winning the Stuyvesant (Bob Coglianese)

Page 14: Slew retires (New York Racing Association); Slew at Spendthrift (Barbara D. Livingston); Slew at Three Chimneys (Dan Johnson)

Page 15: A.P. Indy, Surfside (Barbara D. Livingston); Swale (The Blood-Horse); Slew o' Gold (New York Racing Association)

Page 16: Slew in 2000 (Tony Leonard); Statue at Three Chimneys (Anne M. Eberhardt)

D an Mearns was managing editor of *The Blood-Horse* magazine, editor of *The Florida Horse*, and managing editor of the *Thoroughbred Record*.

A founding member of the Kentucky Thoroughbred Media, he won six Eclipse Awards and eight American Horse Publication Awards. He died in 2022.